11/13/09

Beyond the Rice Paddies

Dear Dave,

Forever Grateful!!

Welcome Home!

LINDA WEST

BEYOND THE RICE PADDIES

2008

Beyond the Rice Paddies

GRATITUDE

Herbert Robert West, my stepfather
U.S. Army
519 Military Intelligence Battalion

Veterans who served in Vietnam

Unsung Heroes
Who continue to save children during times of war.

THANK YOU

Dave Lenckus

I am forever grateful for your encouragement and wonderful editing style.

This Is Dedicated To Ba Noi.

"You are alive in my heart, my mind and my soul. I will forever treasure our time together."

CONTENTS

I see myself as one of the little children, not on the streets of Iraq but in a small village, under a bridge in Bien Hoa, Vietnam.

PROLOGUE
IT ALL COMES BACK

In a matter of a few minutes in the theater, watching a movie bashing George W. Bush, my heart feels a tug. Spots of memories bubble to the surface as I look at the screen into the faces of the little children from Iraq. They are smiling, riding their bikes and walking before the war. Then the scene switches to them playing among the rubble in the midst of war.

I see myself as one of the little children, not on the streets of Iraq but in a small village under a bridge in Bien Hoa, Vietnam.

A couple of months later, I am at a birthday party for a friend, Mike. Dave, my companion, and I are in a light conversation with a man named Al. He is tall and slender, in his late forties to mid-fifties. He has deep brown eyes and a calm, composed disposition. After our conversation, I watch him walk away to join his family on the backyard patio. I feel I must have met him before; where, I cannot recollect.

Renee, Mike's wife, approaches us. With her warm smile and in a cheerful voice she says: "I see you met Al, my brother-in-law. He served in Vietnam. Did you notice his left hand? He was hurt in the war. A hand grenade blew off a few fingers and damaged one of his legs. He received a Purple Heart."

This has never happened to me before. A sudden rush of gratitude overcomes me.

A little later, Dave and I spot Al through the crowd in the

house. I walk over to him and reach for his arm. I whisper to him, "Renee just told us that you were in Vietnam."

He nods yes.

"I know this sounds selfish of me, but thank you for your sacrifices. I am here because of you."

He has a surprised look on his face and says, "Veterans Day was two days ago. But thank you."

A sudden desire to hug him overcomes me, but I don't want him to feel awkward. So I touch his arm and say, "Al, I know, but not just Veterans' Day. I am thanking you for all the days that have made up the last thirty-four years and all the days in my future. I am from Vietnam. Thank you so much. I am here today because of you. I am forever grateful."

For a few seconds, there is silence. Then I look into his eyes, which are so deep, so intense, so captivating and—at that moment—so moist. I am touched to the core of my soul.

Our conversation begins and flows. Al describes to me his troop's marches through the villages; the little Vietnamese children begging for candies; children who were Viet Cong; his troop's searches for the Viet Cong in the rice paddies; the white powder from the airplanes; the explosions; and even his own near death.

Recollections unfold, and some questions I have had are answered. So many years of surreal memories have been tucked away. Day-to-day life in America is what I live and deal with. The necessity of handling changes, opportunities and challenges at present occupy me. No time for the past.

Tears trickle down my cheek as we hug each other. Dave is so gracious to stand by us and allow us to share our stories. Never once, though, did Al mention the Purple Heart he received.

"In more than thirty years, no one has ever come up and thanked me. I am touched. I have wondered how it affected the children. The joy of them running up to us, placing their little hands into our pants pockets for candies. Then it all changed. They ran up to us and placed hand grenades in our pockets. It was necessary then to push them off of us. Some of the guys in the troop used their rifle butts to knock them away. I could never bring myself to do that."

He then squeezes my arms, eyes teary, and walks out the sliding glass door into the night.

I excuse myself and head to the bathroom, where I compose myself and wipe the smeared eyeliner off my face.

As I look into the mirror, I catch a glimpse of a little Vietnamese girl.

All was so glorious to her after arriving in America, living in paradise with so much of everything—wonderful things—and all so nice, crisp and clean. No explosions, no gunfire, and plenty of food, candies, clothes and toys.

It was the fall of 1970, less than a year after we arrived in America, and we were stationed in Indian Head, Maryland. I was at a sleepover at my new friend's house. That night, before we went to sleep, my friend told me her uncle was killed in Vietnam and how awful it has been for her family.

It hit me, head on! The beloved uncle of this sweet new friend of mine—who had invited me into her home and was sharing her bed with me—was killed in Vietnam. What could I do for her? What could I say to comfort her?

From that moment on, being around my friend and her family was difficult for me. I began to believe that any and all association with Vietnam—including me—translated to destruction, death, anger, shame and guilt. Not that I was so significant that I alone could carry the weight of responsibility for such an overwhelming national heartache. But as a child, not knowing how to communicate, the only thing I could do was feel shameful and guilty.

I had to move on, so I buried it all—all of the memories.

Running into Al and seeing the movie footage of the beginning of the Iraq war helped me uproot all of those memories.

Grateful I am to Al for helping me to recognize that my spots of memories aren't illusions. The memories were not implanted in my head from war movies I have seen, and they aren't things I made up.

Finally, I am able to feel that little girl, not just see her as a third person as I had. I am able to accept her, to accept me, and to value the experiences and memories and all the people who were part of them.

The war was part of my daily life as a little girl—many times frightened, many times smiling, many times playing, many times crying and many times wondering.

The war also was part of Al's daily life at one time. I found a haven and comfort with my one angel—my paternal grandmother, my Ba Noi. What or who was Al's haven?

In that different time and place, could Al have seen me as one of the children who placed grenades in American GIs' pockets? I was one of the little children but not one who would even think of stuffing a grenade in their pockets.

Now, this night, thirty-something years later, I hope Al sees me as a woman who is grateful to be alive, to live in a country that allows her to raise three wonderful children.

***

Thank you to all veterans and especially to the Vietnam Veterans of America. From meeting and talking to the veterans, I realize that some of them still carry, daily, the experiences of the horrific actions that were forced upon them. One veteran whom I met at a fundraiser event organized by the VVA clutched onto me as tears of sorrow poured from his eyes. He asked for forgiveness, and my heart just dropped. At that moment, I represented the innocent children whom might have endured the atrocities of war, but he was also a victim of the atrocities. Because of the decency in his heart, he carries those nightmares with him to this day, almost forty years later. And those atrocities carry over to these veterans' loved ones, who endure them enduring these nightmares.

Even with all that haunts that veteran, he expressed to me that we need to help our young soldiers of today—those coming back from Iraq and Afghanistan. "The nightmares will continue," he said. At the same event, another VVA shared with me his heart-rending memories of just a few months ago. He went back to Vietnam with his wife and a few other veterans. They traveled to areas that at another time were killing fields. Now, the fields are filled with life and love. There, he, his wife and other veterans built a school for Vietnamese children.

To these veterans, I want to express my gratitude—both for your great work in Vietnam today and because you made me feel safer in my village when I was a young girl. I want to express my gratitude. I was safe because you came to my village. Thank you.

Thank you to my wonderful stepfather—a young American soldier, just barely twenty years old when he married my mother and adopted me and my two half brothers. I am forever indebted to you.

And finally, honor goes to the mother of my Vietnamese father—my Ba Noi—who nurtured me during my most impressionable years and illustrated how to live life with love and not hate, with compassion and not condemnation. I am so grateful for the seed you planted in me. Your spirit is alive.

Even now when I look at the pictures of the two of us, your love exudes around me, and the smell of jasmine fills the air.

The following chapters are vignettes of my memories from the age of four to ten. Memories of a little girl in a war-torn area of the world, of what she was thinking and feeling as gunfire and dark clouds of death were an everyday event in her country.

In sharing these memories, I hope to inspire others to reflect on the effect of war and its creations that forever change the lives of all within its path. We might not be able to control events that happen, but we can control our actions caused by the events.

My action and commitment is to give something back by donating at least fifty percent of the royalties of this book to the Vietnam Veterans of America and to the Iraq and Afghanistan Veterans of America and to use another portion of the royalties to rebuild a grade school in Vietnam.

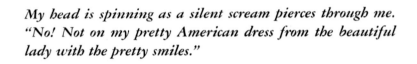

My head is spinning as a silent scream pierces through me. "No! Not on my pretty American dress from the beautiful lady with the pretty smiles."

PRETTY AMERICAN DRESS

Walking to school, I realize that I am late. Normally I would be so afraid. But today, the morning for me moves in slow motion.

I take my time relishing the smell of the morning—the scent of lime trees as I pass by my uncle's lime orchard, the sweet anise in the broth of Pho steaming from the kitchens of the villagers' homes, and the lasting fragrance of my mother's sweet perfume.

The wet dirt road ahead of me appears so smooth. I am amused by the sight of a little man on the back of the muddy water buffalo in the rice paddy.

I take deep breaths—not because I am nervous about what might happen to me for arriving late for school, but for the memory of yesterday.

I feel so elegant, so sweet and pretty in the new dress that my mother gave me yesterday, when she visited me. Her visits are precious treasures to me. She lives in the big city of Saigon, and I see her only two or three times a year. Every visit is pure joy, leaving me with loving thoughts. My mother, the beautiful lady, brings me wonderful gifts: a little American doll with yellow hair, gum, a beautiful American dress, and—most valuable—her pretty smile.

In my head are glistening thoughts of her visit and the pretty dress I'm wearing—not any fear of what might await me as I float to school.

Usually, I would be wearing one of the traditional outfits that my Ba Noi makes especially for me—loose cotton pants with a matching blouse. But today, I am going to school in a beautiful dress made in America.

It is a wonderful style, light yellow, sleeveless, down to my knees and has many pleats. Everything about it is so perfect. The stitching is all the same size and completely straight. The buttons are so evenly spaced apart, and the skirt flares out so beautifully. I just love the new dress that Mother gave me.

The school yard is barren. Everyone is inside, and class has started. Peeking in the doorway of my classroom, I glance at my teacher. Miss Ngyuen is a young woman with a face as flat as rice paper. She has thin pale lips, and her hair is pulled back in a tight bun, which makes her eyes narrow and slanted.

The look on her face is not one of welcome. Miss Nguyen, not the prettiest and certainly not the nicest teacher in our school, asks me, "Why are you late?"

At that moment, I feel goose bumps on the back of my neck and all the way down my back. My legs are shaking. In a very quiet, squeaky voice, I reply, "I don't know, Teacher. I am so sorry."

Miss Nguyen steps to the chalkboard and reaches for the extended wood ruler that is set on a cradle. She turns and asks me to put my palms out.

Panic washes over me. The goose bumps spread across my whole body, and my legs become even more wobbly. The other children, sitting quietly, stare at me.

Oh, the ruler appears so wide. As it strikes my palms, the pain is instant. I try not to cry, but the tears well up and drip down my face. My body shakes. My chin is touching my chest, because I can't look up to see all the eyes upon me.

Then this extremely large hand digs into my forearm. Miss Nguyen drags me out to the lonely dirt schoolyard. Sternly, she tells me to stand next to the flagpole in the middle of the yard

and extend my arms until she comes and tells me, "No more."
She stomps away, and I am alone.

I close my eyes, and more tears drip down my face. I realize
they are falling on my dress. My head is spinning as a silent
scream pierces through me: "No! Not on my pretty American
dress from the beautiful lady with the pretty smiles. No tears,
no tears, no tears, please, on my pretty American dress."

With my eyes still closed, I tell myself: "Stop crying. Don't
let the tears stain the beautiful American dress." I take a deep
breath and savor the scent of the lime orchard, the sweet anise
and my mother's sweet perfume. In my mind, I see Mother's
beautiful smile.

All is calm, peaceful and painless.

His spirit will be in limbo, without a home or hope for an afterlife.

LITTLE BOY

The open market has a concrete floor, big columns at each corner that support a rusted tin roof but no walls. It is rectangular in shape and almost as big as three— or maybe four or five—houses.

In the morning it is vibrant, as people from the village beyond the rice paddies and across the river come to sell their goods. On any morning, you might find bitter melons, large squash, all types of bok choy, lychee, sweet pink grapefruit, live chickens, frogs, fresh fish, duck eggs, rice, spices, fresh herbs, jasmine rice, paper lanterns, incense, natural dried herbs and teas for medicinal healings.

The market always comes alive with sounds of children's laughter, people excitedly and loudly bartering, chickens clucking, ducks quacking, frogs croaking, dogs barking, and babies crying.

But this morning, something is different; the people at the market are subdued and uneasy. There is a crowd gathering in one area. I think I hear some crying and gasping. I start heading toward it, but my Ba Noi takes my hand and tells me it is time for us to go home. I continue to hear crying and gasping as we cross the dirt road to our house.

Within a few hours, all the merchants have packed up their goods, and the open market is empty. From our house, which is directly across from the market, something colorful catches my eyes. I ask Ba Noi if I can go to the market. I think someone has left something there.

Ba Noi sits me down. She looks at me with her big eyes, which have filled with tears. "No, Oanh, don't go across the road to the market. What you see there is the Vietnamese flag; it is covering the body of a little boy about your age. Early this morning, the soldiers dragged his body out from the river. They are hoping that someone will recognize him. But no one has come to claim him, yet."

My eyes, too, become blurry with tears. How sad for this little boy, who is my same age, waiting out in the open market for his family, or someone, to come for him.

The river is where we go to wash our clothes, bathe and play. Ba Noi never lets me go too far out. I wouldn't anyway. The river is so big, and all I can see from the shore is endless murky, brown water.

One time, Aunt Bay took me there with her soon-to-be husband. They laid a blanket on a slope, away from the water, and we sat and ate rice and salty pork. Afterward, Aunt Bay and her soon-to-be husband talked and giggled as they strolled down to the water with a bamboo fishing rod. Aunt Bay allowed me to walk along the river in my bare feet. It was fun to watch the cool mud go between my toes. I hopped and skipped behind Aunt Bay and her soon-to-be husband as we headed home. What a wonderful day! I couldn't wait to show Ba Noi the big ugly fish we caught!

The river of brown water was very friendly that day to us. But the river was not so friendly to this little boy.

"Ba Noi, can we go see him? Maybe I know him. Maybe he is from my school."

"No, some of the teachers from your school have seen him this morning. They do not recognize him."

The rest of the day, my eyes are fixed on the colorful flag

across the dirt road. Normally, there would be a small group of children jumping rope or playing hopscotch or pick-up sticks at the open market. Many times I am there, too, watching them play. Sometimes they let me join in. But, today, no children are playing.

Every now and then, some village people come to look at the body under the red, yellow and green flag, but then they walk away.

It is dinnertime, but I am not able to finish my bowl of rice. All I can do is think about the little boy. I wonder what he looked like. Was he taller or shorter than me? Did he have very dark skin, or was it light like mine? Did he smile a lot, or was he sad and lonely?

The day is almost gone, and night is falling around us. The rain has come, along with roaring thunder and frightening lightning. I wonder if the little boy, like me, was afraid of the thunder and lightning.

I remember one dark and shadowy night when my father was visiting. Ba Noi, my father and I sat around the big round table with some large candles in the middle. Our enormous shadows hovered over us as they mimicked our every movement. One thunder clap was so enormously loud that it made me jump out of my chair, and I let out a scream.

At that instant, my father slapped me across the face, and then a big gust of wind blew out the candles. For a few seconds, my face felt like it was on fire. I started to cry. I tried to understand why my father hit me. My father lit the candles again with the American cigarette lighter that he cherished. When he saw me on the floor under the table crying, he scolded me for being such a crybaby. But Ba Noi came over and circled her arms around me.

Now, the rain and thunder have stopped, and night is

beginning to set in. No moon. No stars. No glimpse of hope for the little boy.

As I go to bed, my heart aches with sadness for him. I should have asked Ba Noi to put a bowl of rice and some fruit out for his journey to the afterlife. It is so upsetting that this little boy cannot start his journey if his family does not come for him. His spirit will be in limbo, without a home or hope for the afterlife.

Just the other day we had a funeral ceremony for one of our friends in the village. Everyone wore white clothing. A parade was given in his honor; rice, fruit and incense were placed by his headstone. I want the same for this lonely boy.

The darkest of night is here. The little boy has to stay out in the big open market all by himself, and I do hope that his family comes for him soon. As I lay in my cozy straw bed, I become frightened thinking about the little boy as a ghost. I hope he doesn't come across the street to our house and give me bruises.

Ghosts have visited me during my sleep before. I had no bruises before going to bed, but when I woke up, there they were on my arms and sometime on my legs. Those ghosts were angry.

I start thinking about the river and what would happen if I drowned. It would be different for me. Vietnamese soldiers live in a compound next to the open market. They see Ba Noi and me every day. They would know who I am and bring me to her. There would be no need to leave me out on the hard concrete.

Ba Noi would prepare me for the funeral ceremony, and there would be plenty of food for my journey.

No, I wouldn't be left out in the dark alone at the market.

Oh, how horrible for the little boy. I wish him a good night and hope that good spirits will watch over him.

Am I dreaming, or is this real? In the middle of the night, the boy is being lifted away. I can't make out the faces around him, but all are very loving and wearing white. They are so gentle with him. No loneliness, no fear for the boy. All bad spirits have been cast away. As the boy floats away, he looks at me, nods his head and gives me a smile. I smile back, and then he and all those in white disappear.

I can sleep now.

Morning has come. I spring out of bed and run to the front of our house to look over at the open market. The little boy and the flag are gone. I wasn't dreaming last night.

He is safe now. His journey has begun, with all those in white surrounding him, guiding him and loving him.

Ba Noi comes beside me, and we both stare in gladness at the empty, concrete ground where once the little boy lay. She closes her eyes, smiles sweetly and softly chants for a wonderful afterlife for the little boy.

My heart is at peace for him.

Goodbye, little boy, goodbye. Onto your journey, onto your afterlife.

I fear the rickety slats underneath my feet will give way and I will fall into the deep pit where all the yucky stuff collects.

HOUSE OF BA NOI

I love the house that Ba Noi and I live in. It is very nice, always clean and not full of things. It is made of thin wooden walls, which is better than some of the houses, made of straw or sheets of rusted tin.

The house is second from the corner of the street. Across the dirt road is the open market, which spreads from the corner of the street to the end of our house.

The compound where the South Vietnamese soldiers live is next to the open market. It is surrounded by a wall of sandbags, one on top of the other. On top of the sand bags are coiled barbed wires. The wall is much higher than me, higher than Ba Noi and higher than my father. There are lookout areas all along the wall.

Something about the back wall of the compound gives me a creepy feeling.

Was there a gun pointing at me from the compound? I think I took the back route from Uncle Hai's house to go home. The soldier shouted at me, but he didn't shoot. Perhaps he recognized me. Was I just dreaming, or did it happen a few weeks, maybe a few months ago? I don't remember.

The front of our house has an area to fix flat bicycle tires. A man in the village comes in the morning and stays until lunch time to help Ba Noi with the work.

Behind the little area for fixing bicycles, there is one big room with a huge table for entertaining family and neighbors.

The people of our village often gather at our house, and many sit around this big round table to eat, laugh, drink and talk for hours. On special celebration days, like Têt, the Lantern Festival, a big wedding, the anniversary of the day that Ong Noi—my grandfather—went to his afterlife, or a funeral ceremony, everyone gathers here, because Ba Noi is the best cook in the whole village.

Separate from the large room is a small private area, where we have an altar for our beloved ancestors. There are small colorful curtains on three sides of this area to separate it from the large room.

The altar is adorned with several statues and pictures of different Buddha, an urn filled with uncooked rice to hold incense, and a bowl filled with fresh fruit. A faded picture of Ong Noi also sits on the altar.

Our sleeping area is in the back of the house. It has a very good roof on it. Ba Noi sleeps on a metal cot with a soft cushion on it. I sleep cattycorner to her on a bed made of wood, which is raised much higher than the cot. My bed is very comfortable with soft straw padding and a few pillows. The nice white cloth nets around our beds keep the big pesky mosquitoes away.

At times when Ba Noi and I are settled in our beds, she tells me stories. My favorite story is the one about a beautiful girl and her two stepsisters and stepmother. The beautiful girl wanted to go to a ball given by the king for his beloved son. The stepmother taunted her. She told the beautiful girl she could go to the ball if she picked up every grain of rice that had been scattered throughout their huge orchard. Millions and millions of grain of rice were strewn across the orchard. The beautiful girl sobbed, because she knew that by the time she picked up every grain of rice, the ball would be over. She felt hopeless, but her friends came to the rescue. Her friends—hundreds of birds and wonderful little creatures—amazingly, within minutes, gathered every grain of rice. She went to the ball and met the young prince. They married and lived happily ever after.

Under my bed is a dugout, wide enough for about three or four people and deep enough that when we sit in it, our heads are below the opening. I don't remember when this was built, but I remember the times we have been in it—when the Viet Cong and the Vietnamese soldiers were fighting around our house and sometimes fired through it.

On one side of the house is the kitchen. It is mostly exposed to the outdoors. Ba Noi cooks wonderful and delicious food here. My favorite is salty pork with boiled eggs over fresh warm white rice. I love it when Ba Noi pours extra sauce from the salty pork over the rice. She also cooks puffy dumplings with incredible meat fillings in the middle, and fried sliced sweet potatoes coated in gooey brown sugar.

In one corner of the kitchen area are two large rectangular concrete water tanks. One tank is for our drinking water, which Ba Noi boils, and the other holds the water we use for washing our hands and dishes.

There are banana and papaya trees just a few feet away from the kitchen. All sorts of herbs, especially mint, grow wildly around the trees and everywhere else. Ba Noi uses the herbs in many of her dishes. I love the mint gelatin and the mint juice. They are so cool and refreshing on hot muggy days.

A few feet away from the kitchen is a vegetable garden. Here, a variety of squash, bitter melons, cabbages and other greens are plentiful.

At times, there are an abundant amount of frogs hopping in and out of the garden, too. They are so slimy and slippery. Trying to catch them is a lot of fun.

Separating the kitchen from the washroom is a heavy cloth curtain. The washroom has a very large concrete holder for water to do our daily washing. Once a week, Ba Noi washes my hair. I love her hands massaging my head, wrapping all of my long hair into one soft clump, on and on. It is so calming and comforting. Afterward, she combs my hair and picks at my scalp to make sure I don't have lice.

The dark and gloomy toilet room is outside at the rear of the house. Inside are two wood planks to squat on. There are only a couple small openings high on the walls for some light to shine through.

I am so fretful when I have to use the toilet, especially when night settles in. I have heard there is a ghost that knows when you are up during the dark of night and have to wander outside to use the toilet. This ghost will follow you and take you away so you will never be found. Where this ghost takes you, know one really knows.

One night I had to go really badly. During the walk from the house to the toilet, all I could think of was the ghost following me. I was so frightened that I ran back to the house. I felt like such a baby, being as scared as I was. But I was a big girl, so I didn't want to bother my Ba Noi with such silly fears. So I went to bed. When I woke up in the night from a dream that I had to use the toilet, I found myself all wet.

Even in the daylight, I hate to use the toilet. Grotesque it is, with all the maggots and big fat flies. The two wood planks do not look very sturdy. I fear that the rickety slats underneath my feet will give way and I will fall into the deep pit where all the yucky stuff collects.

But my fears will end soon.

Today is an exciting day, because we are having a real toilet built! A Modern toilet! No more wood slats. No more maggots. No more big fat flies. I won't have to worry about falling into the bottomless pit.

I can't believe how many people from the village are here.

We are one of the first in the village to have a new modern toilet, and everyone is very curious about how it will look.

It has taken all day for my father, Uncle Hai and a few other men from the village to build this incredible toilet.

Ba Noi, Aunt Bay, my father, Uncle Hai and I marvel at the magnificence of the new modern toilet. No longer are there thin wooden planks to sit on. No longer can you look down into it. There is now a raised concrete platform with a very nice round opening. It has four walls and feels very intimate and private. The tin roof has a little awning attached to it to cover the doorway, so you won't get wet in rainstorms. There is a concrete step to help you get up onto the platform.

We are so proud of this toilet! So proud that we are marking the year it is built—1967—in its fresh wet concrete step.

Yes, a time for celebrating. The people from the village share in our joy, too.

I am happy, happy, happy—a real, modern toilet for us!

She is so endlessly patient—not just with me but also with my father.

BA NOI

Ba Noi is so dear to me. Never does she scold me; always she holds me.

Ba Noi is taller than most other women in the village. She has oval porcelain features, striking high cheek bones, a tall nose and big, round, dark almond eyes. She has beautiful long black hair that she wears in a big round bun.

I cherish her soothing voice and quiet and graceful movements. Her long arms and hands flow in the air as I watch her practice her tai chi every morning.

She is so endlessly patient—not just with me but also with my father. He is much taller than most men in the village. I have been told that I look very much like my father, who I think looks very much like Ba Noi. Yes, father is a handsome man, especially when he wears his dark sunglasses and has a cigarette in his mouth.

When father comes to visit now and then, sometimes he gives me a ride on his amazing motor scooter. It is so much fun feeling the wind in my hair as I stand right in front of him on the foot rests with my hands on the handle bars going faster and faster.

He always asks whether I have been a good girl for Ba Noi. Today, I tell him I have not.

"I try very hard to always be good. The one bad thing I did, which I am sorry for, is that I did not eat my bowl of rice the other day."

Father raises his eye brows and says coldly, "Go On."

I nervously answer: "Aunt Bay was here, and she was very upset at me. She made me sit for hours and hours until I finished my rice. Ba Noi told Aunt Bay that she is worried I am too skinny and sickly. I am sorry to make Ba Noi upset."

"You must try harder to be good."

"Yes, Father, I am very sorry. I will finish all my rice."

I remember Aunt Bay shrieking at me: "For every grain of rice you don't finish is a maggot you have to eat when you go to hell!" Oh, horrible! I will eat all my rice from now on. Yes, Father, I will eat all my rice.

There is no motor scooter ride today. Father came just to talk to Ba Noi about a serious matter. Feeling the importance of it, I am very quiet during their talk. Ba Noi leads father to the back of the house where she and I sleep. On one of the walls are numbers written with white chalk. Most of the numbers have lines through them.

She points to the numbers without the lines and says to him: "See, on the wall? You need to pay those first before you get more money."

Father is very upset with her order and storms out of the house.

***

I sit in the back of the temple by the door and listen to the wonderful, soothing chanting from Ba Noi and the others. The smell of incense drifts through the air. I close my eyes and listen for the sounds of the gong and the subtle rustling of the beads. I do not chant with the others. I just close my eyes and take in all the wonderful sounds and smells.

I fall into a half sleep, feeling light as I float along. Good visions appear. Celebrations, the moon, other children laughing and holding paper lanterns, the glimmer of dancing lights, water flowing in the river as paper boats with small candles float away, the smell of crisp new money in red envelopes for Tet-Chinese Lunar New Year. The man on a water buffalo in the rice paddies, the scent of lime and grapefruit orchards, the aroma of jasmine and blended fresh herbs. The crash of ocean waves, the cool soft sand between my toes, a crab disappearing as it digs itself a hole in the wet sand. A beautiful lady with brownish orange hair and a beautiful smile.

I love the temple. Goodness surrounds us all.

***

We are rushing home after leaving the temple. Today, we are celebrating the afterlife of Ong Noi.

The gravesite of Ong Noi is near our house. It is fairly simple in design. There is a sculpted lotus flower at each corner. Ba Noi told me that one day her gravesite will be next to his, and it too will be of the lotus design.

There are lime and grapefruit trees around the gravesite of Ong Noi. One of the greatest honors and the best way to show respect for your ancestors is to build for them the grandest gravesite or mausoleum. One day when I am a school teacher and have a lot of money, I will build the biggest, most beautiful mausoleum for Ba Noi.

Many members of our family and friends from the village will be joining us to honor and give respect to him. The monks from the temple will be there, too. They'll chant for hours and hours at the ancestral altar.

Ba Noi needs to finish making the most delicious food for the celebration of her departed husband. She is known as the best cook in the whole village. Oh, how delicious! The white doughy buns with minced pork in the middle, and the spring rolls, so perfectly wrapped in delicate rice paper, fried to a light crunch and dipped in the most flavorful fish sauce. She also does wonderful things with the lemon grass, watercress and herbs growing around our house. She has promised that one day she will teach me all her cooking secrets.

Now, we are almost home, so I ask: "Ba Noi, why did Ong Noi leave this life?"

"Child, your Ong Noi started his journey early. He had gone to one of the mountain villages nearby to tell people where one family's land ends and another begins. He was gone too long. I felt something was wrong and went to the temple to chant for him. The next day he came home.

"He told me his trip was not good, and he was feeling very uneasy. Several families in the mountain village were very upset. They did not agree with the map he drew, and they kept arguing with him about where their land begins and ends. Before he headed down the mountain, one old woman approached to scold him. He believed that she went into a trance and placed a bad curse on him.

"After dinner that night, we stayed up a little later than usual. His stomach was very upset, and he broke out in a sweat. It was late into the night before he was able to go to sleep.

"The rooster crowed, and I woke up. Normally, your Ong Noi would wake up right before the rooster crowed, but that morning he didn't. I thought that he was very tired from such a bad trip to the nearby mountain village. Gently, I placed my cheek next to his. How cold he was. During his sleep, he had stopped breathing. Ong Noi had begun his journey to the afterlife. The horrible curse from the old woman in the mountain village was fulfilled."

Every single day I have watched Ba Noi at the ancestral altar in our home. She lights fresh incense and places it into an urn. Then she bows her head, kneels and chants. Sometimes the chants are for only a few minutes; other times she chants for hours. I think that after thanking all the Buddha, she talks to Ong Noi.

What a wonderful wife she is! One day when I am a wife and my husband goes to the afterlife before me, I will talk to him every day, too.

As we approach our house, Aunt Bay, the youngest of Ba Noi's six children and the only girl, runs to greet us. She is pretty, though not as pretty as my mother. Her face is round, big and a little flat instead of small and delicate like my mother's. She always wears her hair down and has a very beautiful sway about her body when she walks. Each step she takes reminds me of one of those elegant ducks in the water.

But she is not as patient as Ba Noi. Several times she has scolded me because I could not read the books she brings for me or I didn't finish my bowl of rice or I wasn't paying attention to her instructions.

I have heard Ba Noi tell Aunt Bay how very proud my aunt makes her. Aunt Bay goes to college and is extremely smart. The man she is to marry comes from a very wealthy family. Ba Noi says that Aunt Bay will not be living with us but with her new husband and his father and mother after they get married.

All girls go to live with their husbands' families and help take care of them. Ba Noi has told me she is proud of me for trying very hard in school. She says I must keep practicing my handwriting. It is getting very pretty. I do enjoy dipping the pen in the black ink and drawing out the words to make them look curvy and elegant.

I will work harder so Ba Noi can be more proud of me, too. One day I will be a school teacher, a nice one. I will be patient like Ba Noi and talk in a soothing voice. I will not shout and make my voice unbearably screechy.

But I don't want to live away from Ba Noi, so when I get married, my husband will come and live with Ba Noi and me. He can help our family.

Today, I am happy to see Aunt Bay. She is so much nicer when we have a celebration.

I could still hear a humming noise coming from the sky, but I could not see anything other than this chalky dust.

BUBBLES

It is so hard for me to wake up for school.

Ba Noi comes to my bed and says, "Oanh, you will be late for school. It is time to get out of bed." She lays her hand on the back of my head and raises me up.

I open my eyes. I feel so weak. All I want to do is lay back down. "Ba Noi, I don't feel good."

"Do you feel any pain?" she asks as she gently raises my right elbow.

I shake my head no. "I feel tired."

"Oanh, look at your arm, your shoulder. They are covered with big clear bubbles, almost like large blisters. Lay back down slowly. They are on your back, too," she says with a worried look on her face.

I look at my right arm. There are clear bubbles from my elbow area up to my shoulder. I can't see the ones on my back. I feel no pain, just weak and uneasy. Looking at them makes me want to scratch and pop them, but at the same time I am afraid. It would hurt if they popped. No, I can't lay back down.

It is known in our village that at times when you are asleep, bad spirits and ghosts can come, touch you, and leave black and blue marks on you. It frightens me to think that many ghosts and spirits came to me last night. But why, instead of black and blue marks, have they left these bubbles on me? How could I have slept through it all? What did I do wrong to deserve this? I don't understand.

Ba Noi soothes me with her soft gentle voice. "Oanh,

child, you are going to be well, do not worry." She wipes my face with a warm wet cloth.

After a while, I am feeling a little better and ready to get out of bed. Ba Noi dresses me, but I can't wear my blouse, because it has sleeves. Ba Noi is afraid for anything to touch the bubbles. So, instead of dressing me in my blouse, she takes a soft cotton shawl from her dresser drawer and slings it over my left shoulder and around my chest, pinning it together under my right armpit.

The noodle soup that Ba Noi has made for me is one of my favorites. The noodles appear delicate and clear, almost like glass, as they simmer in a mild broth. The soup is easy to eat and glides smoothly down my throat. Any soup that Ba Noi makes is very flavorful, but today it tastes bland. After one or two sips, I push the bowl away and ask Ba Noi if I can lay down. I am feeling more tired, and my eyes are not seeing too well, because they are so teary.

"Child, you can rest on my bed. It is lower than yours and will be easier for you to get in and out. But I don't want you to lay down right now until after we visit Mr. Doctor." She instructs me to sit up in bed as she puts several pillows behind my back.

I open my eyes to a refreshing, warm wet wash cloth on my face. Ba Noi is wiping my face and neck and says: "You had a nice short nap. Now, it is time for us to see Mr. Doctor."

Mr. Doctor is a pleasant but funny-looking man. He is shorter than Ba Noi and wears thick, round eyeglasses. When he smiles, he shows big yellow teeth. Even when he doesn't smile, it looks like he is smiling, because his two front teeth stick out way too far.

Mr. Doctor says: "Hmm, not chicken pox, not measles. They look like blisters."

He looks at the other side of my body, my left arm,

shoulder and back. "I don't understand why they are only on one side. These blisters look like it could have been caused by a burn. Did anything happen yesterday that was unusual?"

"No," Ba Noi replies. "She went to school. After school, she came straight home. Before dinner she practiced her penmanship. She finished her rice and helped clean up. We washed our dishes and talked a little before bed."

Did Mr. Doctor say it looked like I was burned? My skin was burned? No, I don't remember being burned. That sounds so painful. I would remember.

Mr. Doctor says: "I don't know what I can do for your grandchild. Just make her comfortable, and don't send her to school. If it gets worse, come back. Let us hope they go away in a few days."

We bid goodbye to Mr. Doctor.

It is evening. A few neighbors and friends have come over. We all sit around the big round table with candles lighting our faces. The shadows on the ground and the walls set an eerie mood. Our neighbors and friends are talking about what could have caused these bubbles.

I pretend not to be frightened as I listen to them tell scary stories of evil spirits. The shadows continue to perform their ghostly dances, which create more creepy thoughts in my head.

Ba Noi says: "No, no, don't scare my grandchild. It is getting late. Time for us to say good night."

Everyone leaves.

Ba Noi and I are getting ready for bed. She gives me a wet wash cloth to wipe my face and neck.

It is most important to have clean feet before getting into bed, so Ba Noi helps me wash them.

The best part of getting ready for bed is having my hair combed. Ba Noi is especially careful tonight not to touch my right shoulder as she combs my hair. I like it better when she doesn't do it so gently. Sometimes my head itches so much that the firmer she combs, the better I feel. This is also a good time to talk and ask the many questions I have.

Ba Noi has told me to be good and not to talk unless I am talked to. But, sometimes at the market I overhear someone talking about something I don't understand, or maybe my school friends or teacher tell me something that is unclear. Ba Noi lets me ask about all these things when we get ready for bed.

Tonight I have only one question, one request. "Ba Noi, do I have to go to sleep tonight? I don't want the bad spirits and ghosts to come. Maybe they will touch me and then my left side will have these bubbles, too. Please, I don't want to go to sleep."

She finishes combing my hair, and then she takes my hands, placing them on her face. "Oanh, child, I will stay up. I will be right here beside you. No bad spirits will come tonight. Tomorrow we will go to the temple to chant."

Ba Noi gives me her pillows to support my body so I do not lie on the bubbles. She blows out the candle and lays next to me.

I try my hardest to keep my eyes open. I have to stay awake; I don't want the bad spirits or ghosts to come again. I put many thoughts in my mind. I am thinking of the beach, the little sand crabs and the woman with the beautiful smile— my mother. I think about the man on the water buffalo in the rice paddy whom I always see when I walk to school. I think about the scent from the orchard, my uncle's orchard, with the wonderful smells of fresh limes and large pink grapefruits.

I remember I can't go to sleep. I panic and quickly open my eyes. There is the face of Ba Noi next to mine, her eyes wide open. She says: "It is safe, child. Go to sleep. I am here. Good spirits are here with us."

I close my eyes, than open then again. Ba Noi is serenely watching me, still. She touches my face gently and starts chanting, very softly, very soothingly. The chant sounds like a lullaby, which can only be sung by her. The light scent of jasmine slowly fills my head. Yes, good spirits are with us. It is safe to go to sleep.

Morning is here already. Oh, no! I fell asleep. Did more ghosts come in the night? What about my other arm? Are there bubbles there, too? No, it looks like the bubbles haven't spread. Good spirits are with us.

Ba Noi reminds me that today we are going to the temple to chant. We will chant for the good spirits to take the bubbles away. She is not worried. I am not worried. Good spirits did come last night and protected us. We will chant for good spirits to come and take the bubbles away.

On our way to the temple, I am thinking about school. It has been several days now since I was last at the playground.

I remember that my school friends and I were playing jump rope in the schoolyard. Next to us, another group was playing pickup sticks. Some of the boys were kicking a ball around. We love our break time. After so many days of rain, that day was a treat. A little sunray was filtering through the clouds.

Then we heard the loud, coarse, rhythmic noise from a big green helicopter above us. Some of us looked up to the sky and waved to the soldiers—a few Americans and a Vietnamese man—in the helicopter.

I don't remember why I walked away from the girls jumping rope to wander off by myself. I found myself a little bit beyond the schoolyard, closer to the open fields and rice paddies, when suddenly I heard a different loud noise above me. It wasn't the familiar coarse rhythm of the helicopters. I looked up and saw a large cloud of white, chalky, powdery dust high up in the sky. I could still hear a humming

*noise coming from the sky, but I could not see anything other than this
chalky dust.*

*Then, from a great distance, our teacher commanded all of us to
come back inside. "Quickly, it is time to go inside! Quickly!"*

Break time was over. Back to class again.

Today, the temple is mostly empty. Ba Noi is talking to
one of the monks as I wait in the garden by a pond. I love
watching the big colorful fish in the pretty pond with lotus
flowers floating around. I sit and close my eyes. Nothing comes
to mind.

The sweet smell of incense drifts to the garden. It forms a
big, puffy cloud, which lightly lifts me up and carries me away.

I feel a tap on my cheek, and I open my eyes. It is Ba Noi.
She already has chanted and paid respect to the monks. It is
time to go home.

***

Another day has passed, but still the bubbles are on me.
Those with the liquid have burst. But a lot of them remain
puffy, and the skin around the bubbles looks pretty red. They
itch, and it is driving me crazy.

When we were at the temple, Ba Noi requested that the
monks come to our house. They will be here today and bring
good spirits with them. She feels certain they will be able to
cure me.

It is mid morning, and two monks from the temple arrive.
They have beautiful smooth faces, shiny bald heads and large
black eyes. They are dressed in bright gold gowns that flow
down to their toes. As I follow the monks to the mango tree, I
find myself mesmerized by their graceful movements. It is like
they are floating on air.

The monks have me sit on a small wooden chair under

the big branches of the green mango tree in front of our home. The aroma from the incense, the tempo of their chants, and the rustling of beads are very serene and calming.

The echo of the gong awakens me. The monks are gazing at me with their huge, black, shiny eyes and warm smiles. Ba Noi and the monks speak softly. She then graciously thanks them and bids them goodbye.

Slowly, I lower my eyes to my right arm; all the bubbles are still there.

Ba Noi helps me get up from the chair. In her soft voice she says: "Child, have faith. The bubbles will go away very soon. Don't worry, they will all go away."

The rest of the day, I am anxious, watching the bubbles on my arm as I read a book, as I eat sweet bean pudding that Ba Noi had made, as I finish my bowl of rice with salty pork at dinner. I am still watching and waiting for them to go away, but the night settles in, and yet still they are on me.

Sleepiness overtakes me.

I awake with the face of Ba Noi smiling down at me. We both look at my arm and shoulder; all the bubbles have gone away during the night. Ba Noi sheds happy tears and gives me a huge hug.

I start crying, because I am happy, too.

We must go to the temple and pay homage to the monks.

The villagers were warned that the same would happen to them if they betrayed the Viet Cong.

WHO ARE THE VIET CONG

One, two, three, come in with me.

A few friends and I are playing jump rope at the open market. We stay far away from the dead Viet Cong who has been placed in the market for his family to claim him.

Earlier today, Ba Noi told me that one of the South Vietnamese soldiers from the compound across the dirt road had recognized the dead Viet Cong. He was a son of a family who lives in our village.

I don't understand. Why would he be a Viet Cong? I thought a Viet Cong is from the north and is a Communist, one of the bad people.

Ba Noi explained to me that the government in North Vietnam thinks differently than the government in South Vietnam. Because of this, they fight. Ho Chi Minh is the leader of North Vietnam, and he has many people who believe the same things he does. But she said many people who live in South Vietnam also believe the same thing as the leader of the North. These South Vietnamese believe so much like this leader that they would leave their families and friends and go fight with him. They are the Viet Cong.

Just the other day, Ba Noi saw the young man—the dead Viet Cong—shopping at the open market. She talked to him and asked how his father was doing. She thought he was buying food and supplies for his family, but now she thinks he actually was buying for other Viet Cong beyond the rice paddies. She said he was so polite and always respectful to her.

Her heart was bleeding for him and his family. She closed her eyes and, in a whisper, chanted for him.

I remember, yes, it was at the open market where I heard an awful story about the Viet Cong. It was so very scary that it gave me bad dreams.

A man said that the Viet Cong had heard that the father of a family in our village had disclosed their hideout to the South Vietnamese soldiers. So, the Viet Cong burst into the family's home at dinnertime and dragged the father out of the house.

In front of the man's family, the Viet Cong cut off his head. As blood spurted on the wife and children, the Viet Cong fiercely instructed the family to tell everyone in the village why the father was killed. The villagers were warned that the same would happen to them if they betrayed the Viet Cong.

Could this nice young man be one of the Viet Cong who cut off the head of that father?

Ba Noi told me that from this day on to listen more and talk less, wherever I am. I nodded my head as if this made sense and I understood. She said we need to be careful, because we don't know who the enemy is anymore. She told me not to wander off and to stay in her sight always.

There he lays, not a flag draped over his body but a torn cloth soaked with dried blood. The cloth is too small. It covers only his face, chest and stomach. His sides, arms and feet—all swollen, black and blue—are bulging out from under the cloth. Oh, he smells rotten!

The stench is getting to us. It makes me and the other children want to throw up. Let us not go any closer.

We head farther away and farther away, and we continue to play…one, two, three, jump in with me.…

***

On this second day, the sound of silence echoes throughout the whole village as the open market remains empty, except for the Viet Cong. There he lays with flies buzzing around him.

Some of the other children and I are even more curious. Even though we are fearful of his ghost, we can't help ourselves. We want to get closer and take a peek at him.

Yuck! The smell, the smell! It is worse today. It makes us gag.

But, still we are curious. Closer and closer we get. He is like a dead fish, a very smelly dead fish. I want to run away from him, but I can't. Together, the other children and I continue moving one tiny step at a time toward him.

Our curiosity is disrupted when we hear the voice of Ba Noi. She runs toward us from the house. We knew we were not to be close to this dead Viet Cong. The other children run off as she comes for me.

Rarely does she yell at me. But she is pointing her finger, so I know she is very angry with me. She had told me not to go over to the open market to play, but I have disobeyed her.

As she approaches, I lower my head. In a low voice I say, "Ba Noi, I am very sorry I have disobeyed you."

She takes my hand and we head toward our house.

I ask, "Ba Noi, why is the Viet Cong still at the market? The little boy who drowned in the river was there only for one night. Have the soldiers told the Viet Cong's family he is out here all by himself on the cold concrete floor?"

"I don't think they will be coming for him," Ba Noi answers. "His family feels he has disgraced them by joining the Viet Cong. The soldiers put the body out there knowing that he would not be claimed by his own family. They want to send a message and teach everyone in the village not to shame your family by joining the enemy. They will be taking his body away soon, very soon."

She stops walking and looks firmly down at me. "Child, listen to me. Never play in the area where his body is. His spirit is angry. Angry spirits do angry things. Promise me you will stay away from there."

I bow my head, "Yes, Ba Noi. I promise."

I squeeze her hand as goose bumps spread across my body.

It didn't show, I don't think, but I was terrified, and my heart was beating wildly when the other children and I were inching closer and closer to the horrible, smelly, bloated, dead body. The truth is I am so relieved that Ba Noi came for me.

"Ba Noi, I did not sleep well last night. The thought of the dead Viet Cong frightened me. I even thought I heard the Viet Cong behind our wall. I knew it was all in my head, because you would have told me to drop into the dugout.

"Sometimes, I dozed off and had weird dreams. One dream felt so real. The little boy who drowned was dressed in white and was playing marbles at the same spot where he laid after the soldiers pulled his body out of the brown murky river. As I came closer to him, he looked up at me, and there was this beautiful rainbow glowing just above his head. He smiled. I smiled back.

"Then suddenly a huge, scary, faceless Viet Cong dressed in black and holding the biggest, shimmering machete towered behind the little boy. My body jolted, my legs thrashed, my heart raced wildly. I woke up. No, Ba Noi, I will not play there. Angry spirits are evil."

Nodding her head and still holding my hand, she leads me away from the market, away from the dead Viet Cong.

"Ba Noi, I sorry. I wanted to play with the children and

disobeyed you. Also, I promise never to shame or dishonor our family."

Again, she nods her head, but this time, she gives me a smile of approval.

Dishonoring your family is not a good thing. I love my Ba Noi and would never want to do that to our family. I know that I am too young, but when I am thirteen or so, Ba Noi won't have to worry about me joining the enemy. I want to make her as proud of me as she is of my Aunt Bay—or even prouder. I am going to college and will become a nice teacher, not a mean one.

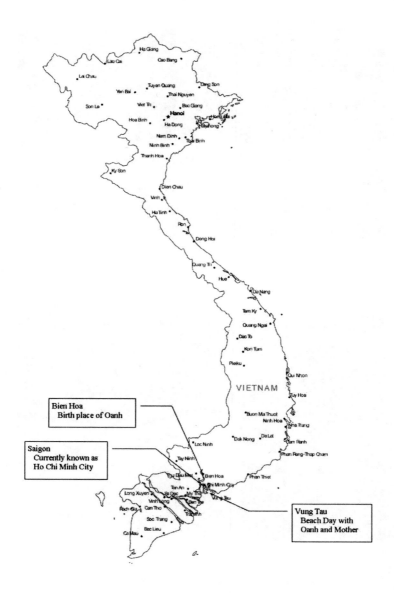

Ha Giang
Lao Cai
Cao Bang
Lai Chau
Tuyen Quang
Dong Son
Yen Bai
Thai Nguyen
Son La
Viet Tri
Bac Giang
Hoa Binh
Hanoi
Ha Dong
Hong Gai
Hai Phong
Nam Dinh
Thai Binh
Ninh Binh
Thanh Hoa
Ky Son
Dien Chau
Vinh
Ha Tinh
Ron
Dong Hoi
Quang Tri
Hue
Da Nang
Tam Ky
Quang Ngai
Dac To
Kon Tum
Pleiku
Qui Nhon
VIETNAM
Tuy Hoa
Buon Ma Thuot
Ninh Hoa
Nha Trang
Dak Nong
Da Lat
Loc Ninh
Cam Ranh
Tay Ninh
Phan Rang-Thap Cham
Thu Dau Mot
Bien Hoa
Ton An
Phan Thiet
Long Xuyen
Sa Dec
My Tho
Ho Chi Minh City
Vinh Long
Ben Tre
Vung Tau
Rach Gia
Can Tho
Tra Vinh
Soc Trang
Bac Lieu
Ca Mau

Bien Hoa
   Birth place of Oanh

Saigon
   Currently known as
   Ho Chi Minh City

Vung Tau
   Beach Day with
   Oanh and Mother

Grade School of Oanh - Hiep Hoa, Bien Hoa, Vietnam

Oanh's grade school, Hiep Hoa, in Bien Hoa, Vietnam.

Classroom of Oanh

Oanh's classroom.

New Modern Toilet—Built 1967

Modern toilet, built in 1967.

Orchard by River of Uncle Hai - 1993

Orchard and pond of Uncle Ba.

Murky, Brown River—Bien Hoa, Vietnam

The murky brown river that claimed the life of the little boy.

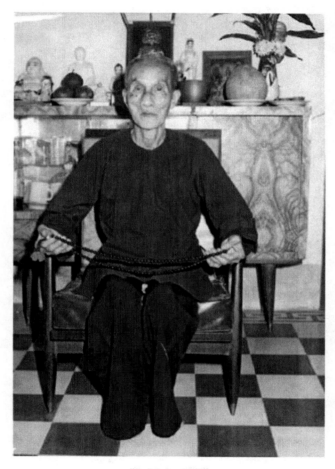

Ba Noi—1993

My Ba Noi, the mother of my father.

Gravesite of Ong Noi

The gravesite of Ong Noi, the father of my father.

Gravesite of Ong Noi and Future Gravesite of Ba Noi—1993

The gravesite of Ba Noi was built a few years prior to her
journey to the afterlife.

Mother and Oanh at the House of Ba Ngoai and Ong Ngoai—1960's

Mother and Oanh in the orchard of Ong Ngoai and Ba Ngoai.

Oanh and Ba Noi - 1993

Oanh returns to Vietnam in 1995 to visit Ba Noi.

Being so close to the Americans is uncomfortable, but Ba Noi is only a short distance from me.

A VISIT FROM THE AMERICANS

I have been anxious for a few days now.

Ba Noi has told me that a group of American soldiers will be across the dirt road at the compound where the Vietnamese soldiers live. The Americans are coming to give all the little children in the village medical checkups to keep us healthy. Ba Noi wants us to be one of the first in line.

The Americans arrive early in the morning. All the children in the village are there, some younger than me, some older. We are very excited.

Ba Noi and I are the first in line, but a few of the other children are restless and push in front of us. I am fine with that, because now I am little afraid of the Americans. Most of them are like giants. The Vietnamese soldiers helping them look like little children.

I stand behind Ba Noi and poke my head out and watch curiously as the Americans signal Minh, a boy older than me who goes to my school, to come to them.

A very tall, slender and pretty Vietnamese lady with beautiful, shiny black hair down to her lower back and wearing a traditional white ao yao asks Minh's mother some questions. The pretty lady then translates the answers for the Americans.

Minh steps up to one of the Americans, who looks into Minh's ears, eyes and mouth and says something to him in Vietnamese.

He lets out a cry as the American pushes a long needle into his skin. I think I am going to be sick. I'm feeling dizzy.

Minh now moves to the next American, who hands him a toothbrush and candies. Oh goodie, I think I can go through the line. It really doesn't look all that bad.

Being so close to the Americans is uncomfortable, but Ba Noi is only a short distance from me. I turn to her and she nods her head, indicating that everything is fine. She tells me to pay close attention to Miss Le and to follow her instructions.

Up close, Miss Le is even prettier. She speaks very properly, like my Aunt Bay. I think she must have gone to a higher level of school just like Aunt Bay. I am in awe, though, when she speaks English. Back and forth she talks to my Ba Noi and then to the American next to her.

Miss Le gives me a sweet smile. She is so elegant and graceful! Her face is delicate porcelain like my Ba Noi's. One day, I hope I can look like her. Still smiling, she looks straight into my eyes and explains what the giant Americans will be doing. Nothing to be afraid of. I will feel a little pinch, like an ant bite. I nod that I understand.

Miss Le instructs me to move forward to the first American. I take a few half steps toward him. He says hello in Vietnamese. I feel timid, a little nervous. He signals for me to come closer. I can do it. There, one more step.

Everything about him is gigantic. Gigantic head, gigantic eyes, gigantic nose, gigantic arms, and gigantic hands! His hand, which is bigger than my whole face, reaches for my right hand. He shakes it and says hello again in Vietnamese. I nod hello back.

He looks into my eyes, ears and mouth. I'm mesmerized by his tangerine hair, the biggest, tallest nose, and little brownish orange spots all over his face. His big eyes are so unusual. They are deeply set with the longest and thickest orange lashes, and they are the strangest color, a weird blue.

He murmurs something in English to Miss Le.

She looks at me and says, "He said you have the prettiest, biggest almond eyes and that you are going to be a very beautiful young lady."

With my head down and looking at the floor, I see big black shiny boots, the largest I have ever seen—maybe five or six times bigger than my feet. Without raising my head, I nod, lift my eyes up and give him just a little smile.

Before I can say thank you, I feel a tiny painful pinch. Ouch! The long shiny needle pokes my left arm. As he removes the needle from my arm, the American looks at me with a grand smile, showing his gleaming, perfect white teeth.

Oh, that was fast. It wasn't all that bad.

I go to the next American. Goodie! He hands me the new toothbrush, a nice little plastic tube of something and candies. He has a grand smile that shows his gleaming, perfect white teeth, too.

Most of the people in the village have yellow teeth. Some of the elders have black teeth from chewing that nasty tobacco. Even worse, some elders do not have any teeth at all.

Maybe if I use the toothbrush that he gave me, I'll have white teeth too. No, this toothbrush is packaged so pretty. I think I am going to put it in my box of treasures.

I like the Americans. They are very nice and always smiling.

In a most monstrous voice, she says something about my mother working in Saigon...

GIRL NEXT DOOR

Mai, an older girl who lives next door, plays with me now and then. Today, I am at her house. We are playing pickup sticks.

Her family is from China, and it is known in the village that they are rich.

I heard some grownups talk one time about how most of the Chinese in Vietnam are very wealthy. I can see that Mai's family is. They own a store that carries all sorts of things: rice, soy sauce, fish sauce, dried seasonings, dried mushrooms, tea, seaweed, flour, sugar, noodles, ointment for pain and fever, Chinese herbal medicine, hairbrushes, barrettes, clothes, paper, writing pens, ink, some toys and games. Sometimes her father lets us play with some of the toys in the store.

Their store also has a special glass case with a lock on it. In this case, all the precious and expensive goods are held, such as a pack of American cigarettes and a lighter, an American watch with "Timex" printed on it, gold bracelets, gold necklaces, a couple of jade Buddha pendants and medicine.

Mai is so lucky. She lives in a huge house. The front of the house is the store; both her mother and father live with her in the back. Theirs is the pretty corner house directly across the dirt road from the open market.

Mai and her family have such beautiful furniture from China. Mai's bed is so soft and comfortable, much more so than my bed with its thin straw mattress.

I think it is mean that some of the other children sing a

song about Chinese people. It goes like this: "Every Chinese is like the other. The ones that give me trouble, I will kick them back to China."

Mai's father and mother are always so polite to Ba Noi and me. I like Mai and her family very much and will not sing that song about them.

I shared with Mai a piece of American chewing gum that my mother, the beautiful lady with the wonderful, sweet, flowery smell and the prettiest smile, had given me. She knows my mother lives in the big city of Saigon and visits me a few times a year. Mai and her mother and father always stare at our house when my mother visits.

Today, I am very excited to show Mai the beautiful new American dress I have on. It comes down to my knees, gathers around the waist and is light blue with little flowers around the bottom. It is especially precious because it was a gift from my mother.

I don't understand. Mai pushes me away from her and tries to pull the dress off me. I am so hurt and shocked; I don't know what to do. I would never try to tear her clothes. She wears such beautiful clothes all the time. I especially like the bright, colorful traditional Chinese outfits made of silk. When she shows them to me, I always ask if I can touch them. The silk feels so cool and smooth.

She pushes me away again and tells me that my dress is very ugly. In a most monstrous voice, she says something about my mother working in Saigon as a bargirl. She also says my mother sells her body to American GIs for money.

What is she talking about? What is a bargirl? How does one sell her body?

Mai continues shouting at me about how the whole village knows what my mother does. She says everyone talks about it. She says I should be ashamed of my mother and myself.

No one has said anything to me about my mother. If there were anything wrong, Ba Noi would have told me.

I want to run away from Mai. I try to lift my feet off the ground, but they are cemented to the floor. Finally, my body listens to me; I am able to turn away from her. All I want to do is go home, but she shoves her face next to mine, spits at me and grabs my dress, trying to tear it.

She starts yelling at me. "You are a daughter of a bargirl. Your mother is a bargirl. The reason you are living with your Ba Noi is because your father is ashamed of your mother. Your mother is a bargirl. I know how she got that dress."

My eyes are filling up with tears, and I can't really see her. Her mouth keeps opening and closing, but I hear no more. Each word from her is sizzling fire from a dragon, burning every part of me.

At last, my legs are strong and I am able to move my cemented feet. As fast as I can, I run. Tears roll down my face, and I cannot see where I am running. I stumble on something and fall to the ground. I just lay there and cry.

Mai is so cruel making up all these lies. I hate her. I hate her. I want to kick her back to China.

Something inside me tells me that whatever a bargirl is, it is not good.

BAR GIRL

"Ba Noi, Mai said I should be ashamed of my mother and myself because my mother is a bargirl. What is a bargirl?"

"Oanh, child, there is much to explain—too much for a little girl to understand. Your mother has a good heart. She is respectful to me. Does she not come to visit you, always bringing you gifts?"

I nod my head yes.

I love the gifts my mother brings me, but most of all I love just being with her. I keep a couple of hair barrettes, a small American doll with yellow hair, a stash of American gum, and a picture of my beautiful mother with light brown hair in the special round tin treasure chest that she also gave me. I wish she could stay longer when she visits, or even better, sleep overnight with us, but she always says she has to go back to Saigon for work.

Once, she brought me back to Saigon with her for a short visit and took me to see her workplace.

There are no windows at my mother's workplace, so it is pretty dark in there. It was fun, because there was Vietnamese and American music playing on a big radio. Mother tried teaching me how to dance to the music.

I sat on a tall chair that spun around, and the man behind the high table gave me a sweet drink. Mother told me that the man behind the table and friends of hers at her work think I am the prettiest girl and very well-behaved.

"Ba Noi," I ask as my eyes become a little moist, "what is a bargirl?" Something inside me tells me that whatever a bargirl is, it is not good.

Ba Noi places my head on her shoulder and pats my back. "No matter what your mother does, remember she loves you very much."

I beg Ba Noi, "Please, tell me what a bargirl is."

Ba Noi lifts my head from her shoulder. My tears have soaked through her blouse. "A bargirl is a woman who works in a place where American men or soldiers come to drink and relax. There is loud music and dancing in this place. The more drinks a bargirl gets the American soldiers to buy, the more money she makes."

I look at Ba Noi, wipe the tears off my cheeks, and sigh with relief. "Ba Noi, I don't think I should be ashamed of my mother for doing that. It doesn't sound bad. I have been at my mother's work. There were no American soldiers there—just a nice Vietnamese man, behind the counter, who gave me a sweet drink that tickled my throat."

Ba Noi squeezes me gently and gives me a half smile. She starts to say something but stops. She squeezes me again and pats my head. "Child, don't be sad, don't be hurt. Forgive Mai. She is only a child herself and does not know everything. Be prepared that others might say hurtful things to you, too. But don't be hurt, don't be sad, don't be angry. Allow your heart to always forgive. Chant, and forgive, so you may move forth with goodness and love."

"Yes, Ba Noi. I will try to forgive Mai. I felt hate in my heart, I wanted to kick her back to China."

"No, Oanh, let go of the hate. Be kind and mindful to your heart. Know that your mother has a kind heart and is very respectful to others. She is always welcome in our home."

I wrap my arms around Ba Noi. Jasmine fills the air.

***

In bed, I think about what happened today. The images appear in my mind. Mai, so ugly, pulls my dress, tries to tear it off me. Mai, looks like the ugliest dragon, fire coming out of her mouth as she spits out nasty words about my mother. Mai and her big, filthy mouth disappear as a bigger and uglier dragon swallows her up.

I am falling, falling asleep as I chant to Buddha to allow my heart to forgive. I also chant to Buddha to help my mother with her work. I hope she gets many men to buy many drinks. One day, she will have a lot of money. Then when she comes to visit, she can stay longer; she can sleep with me on my bed.

As I sleep, I dream. The dream is hazy. Was I with my mother in a room? There is a see-through curtain that separates my mat from my mother's bed. There is a very tall American man with tangerine hair in our room. Soft giggles play in my head. I turn my back to the curtain and close my eyes tight. The soft voices on the other side of the curtain fade away. Curled up on my mat, I sleep.

I knew right away they were Viet Cong, so I quickly ran away.

DUNG—BROTHER

It has been raining for days and days and days. Finally, today is clear.

The man who fixes bicycles at the front of our house arrives. I usually just watch him from a short distance, quietly. It amazes me how fast he can remove the rubber tube from the tire and, within seconds, put it all back together.

One time, the man was busy doing something else and left his tools out. I was curious and went over and picked up some of the tools. The pump was the most interesting one. Each time I pushed the handle down, it made this squeaky noise, and air came out. I knew he used this tool to make the tires big again.

He had a little hammer there, too. I picked it up and banged it on the floor several times. Suddenly, I felt a very sharp pain. I don't know how this happened, but I had hit my nose with it. Ouch! Ouch! Ouch!

My thought of the pain has been interrupted. Ba Noi must have called for me several times, because finally I look up and there she is. Her face is only a hair away from mine.

"Oanh, Oanh, child, can you hear me?"

"Yes, I am sorry, Ba Noi; I was thinking about something."

"This is your older brother, Dung."

There, smiling in front of me is this older boy with dark brown skin and very small slanted eyes.

Ba Noi repeats herself: "Oanh, This is your older brother, Dung. He came all this way to visit you."

I look at him not knowing what to say. So I say nothing.

Dung says: "I am happy to see you. Do you remember me?"

I shake my head no.

"We lived together for a short while at the house of Uncle Ba with Mother and Ba Ngoai," he continues.

Again, I shake my head no.

"It is alright. You were only a couple years old at the time. Do you remember Yen, our sister?"

Again, I shake my head no.

Dung starts to say something, but Ba Noi interrupts him and asks: "Dung, are you thirsty? Would you like something to drink?"

He gives her the biggest smile and nods yes.

She walks toward the kitchen and leaves us both standing there alone.

I say nothing.

He smiles at me and taps me on the arm. "Little Sister, it is no problem. You were so young. I understand if you don't remember me. I live mostly with Ba Ngoai and Ong Ngoai, the mother and father of our mother, across the big river."

I don't remember Ba Ngoai or Ong Ngoai, either.

He continues. "But I come and go whenever I want. Our Uncle Ba has a very nice house close to the beach in Vung Tau. I am on my way to visit him."

Ba Noi walks in with a couple glasses of cool mint juice. Dung quickly grabs one and gulps it down. He hands the empty glass back to Ba Noi, saying, "Thank you."

Ba Noi asks him, "Did I hear you say you are going to visit your uncle in Vung Tau?"

"Yes, I am going to take the train to Vung Tau. I have a funny story to tell. I was just wandering a little way beyond the orchard of the father and mother of our Mother, my Ba Ngoai and Ong Ngoai, when I came across a group of people camping out in the fields. Some of them were carrying big long guns. I knew right away they were Viet Cong, so I quickly ran away. A couple of them were chasing after me.

"As I came closer to our house, I was yelling out, 'The Viet Cong are coming, the Viet Cong are coming.' I knew I was too fast for them, because when I looked back, there was no one behind me. But Ba Ngoai is very worried. She thinks they will come back for me. So she told me, for now, I need to go and live with our uncle in Vung Tau."

Ba Noi agrees with our Ba Ngoai, "Yes, you must go."

"I am not afraid. When I am fifteen years old, I will join the army and fight these Viet Cong," he states in a loud voice.

"Child, be very mindful of what you say to others. It is best to listen more and say less." Ba Noi hands him a little container. "I packed a little food for you."

He thanks her and turns to me with a big crooked smile.

"Little Sister, take care of yourself. I will come back to visit you again. Be good for your Ba Noi and don't cry too much." He gently pats my head and looks at me for a few—but very long—seconds.

I still say nothing. I just nod my head yes.

Turning to Ba Noi, Dung bows to her. With a warm smile, she nods her head. He turns and walks away.

A part of me wants to run after him and ask him to stay longer, but my legs will not listen to my heart. So I just gaze out the dirt road until he disappears. At last, my legs listen to me, and I step out in front of our home. I raise my right arm and wave goodbye.

When he found you, both you and your sister were sickly.

YEN—LITTLE SISTER

I love Ba Noi, but sometimes when the other little children in the village are with their mothers at the open market or at a celebration, I wish I were with my mother, too.

I have been feeling mixed up and lost since the other day when my brother came to visit. I don't remember him at all. We don't look anything alike, and I don't remember living in Vung Tau. I adore my mother and think of her each and every day. Surely I would remember if we had all lived together as he said.

And who is Yen, our sister?

So many questions I have. But I was so stunned when he was here, I couldn't open my mouth to utter even one word.

At times, when something bothers me, I sit as a lotus, smell the incense and listen to my breathing. Nice thoughts come to mind.

Long ago, when we were at the temple, Ba Noi taught me to sit still. By watching her, she showed me how to sit as a lotus, like one of the beautiful pink flowers floating in the pond outside in the temple garden. I did exactly what Ba Noi did. I placed my left foot on my right thigh, my right foot on my left thigh, with my back straight. Then I placed my left hand, palm side up, in my right palm. She had a half smile on her face, and she appeared tranquil and peaceful as her eyes looked straight at the incense in front of us. Her breathing was very slow and relaxing. We sat as lotuses for quite a long time.

Walking home from the temple, Ba Noi asked me what I was thinking when I sat as a lotus. I told her I was thinking of many things. She said, next time, let go of everything and think of nothing.

*I have tried to think of nothing, but always something pops up
in my mind. I begin to relish being a lotus, because I can remember
things—nice things—that happened long ago.*

Since my older brother was here, I have sat as a lotus many
times, digging deep into my mind for memories of all of us
living together in Vung Tau and of my little sister, Yen. Why
can't I remember? Tonight, before bed, I must ask Ba Noi.

"Ba Noi, please help," I plead. "Please tell me about my
brother. He said we have a sister, Yen. I am so mixed up. I don't
remember living away from you. I don't remember him or Ba
Ngoai or Vung Tau or a little sister named Yen."

Ba Noi takes my hands in hers, looks into my eyes and
begins. "Yes, you had a sister. Your father and mother had you
and Yen; she was one year younger than you. Your brother,
Dung, was five or six years old when your father met your
mother. Dung lived with your Ba Ngoai but occasionally would
visit all of you. You and Yen lived with your mother and father
in Bien Hoa, closer to the airport where your father works.

"Your father, my son, I love him dearly, did not do right
with your mother. He had another wife, his first wife, same
wife with whom he now lives."

I do know about my father's wife and their children. My
step-brothers and step-sisters are so lucky. I am jealous of them.
All of them live together near the airport over the bridge in
Bien Hoa. I see them only at some of the celebrations. They
don't talk much to me.

Ba Noi continues. "Because of your father's first wife, your
mother had no place here with your father. She left with you,
Yen and your brother. You all went to Vung Tau and stayed
there with her brother. I think your Ba Ngoai was there, too.
Then she moved you all to Saigon."

I do know Saigon. I don't remember living there, but I
know I have been there. One time when Mother had come to

visit, she asked Ba Noi if I could stay with her for a day or two. Ba Noi looked sad when I left. But I came back and she looked sad no more.

"It was in Saigon where your father found you and brought you here to live with me. He had heard that your mother was working in Saigon. When he found you, both you and your sister were very sickly. You both had stomach problems. Even though Yen was younger than you, she was bigger and looked healthier than you. You were so thin and fragile. It was a shock for all of us that Yen didn't make it through the illness."

Ba Noi stops talking and holds me close. My eyes are moist. I start to miss my sister.

Oh, how wonderful it would be, Yen and I together here with Ba Noi. We could play together, walk to school together, talk to each other before we fall asleep on the same straw bed.

I miss my sister.

Ba Noi asks me: "Are you ok? Do you want to hear more?"

I nod yes.

She continues. "You both were sleeping on the same bed as she went to the light. With Buddha as her guide, she went to her afterlife. We were all very sad, because we wanted to know her better, to know her longer. But good karma will follow her, because she was so young, beautiful and spirited. It was after Yen went to her afterlife that your father brought you here to live with me."

I feel sad, very sad. I want to know her, too.

Ba Noi holds me closer and whispers to me: "Oanh, I know you are sad. Your sister is with us. She is still with us in our hearts, in our minds. I am here with you, too. I will take care of you, child. Ba Noi will take care of you. You will not be alone."

Sitting in the dugout, I can hear the voices and rustling and scuffling of the Viet Cong's movements.

VIET CONG BEHIND OUR HOUSE

I wake up to loud, screeching voices, scurrying footsteps and deafening gunfire.

This is not the first time, so I know the drill. Don't panic, don't get scared, and don't scream. Just roll until I am at the edge of the bed, swing my legs down and then fall into the damp dugout—the hole in the ground under my bed.

The Viet Cong have been behind our walls before. Sometimes in the night, bullets fly back and forth between them and the South Vietnamese soldiers who live across the dirt road from our house.

Those nights, Ba Noi and I sit together in the dugout until morning, when the fighting stops.

But, the damp dirt of the dugout gives me scary thoughts. Some nights, if I think about the dugout under my bed, I get nightmares. I dream that I am in the dugout and the Viet Cong are putting dirt on me and burying me alive.

Now, I slip into the dugout. Oh, the noises. They are so unbearable. Be patient, very still and quiet. Wait for a minute or so, and Ba Noi will roll off her cot to the dirt floor. On her stomach, she will crawl with her elbows to meet me here, where we will be safe together.

Sitting in the dugout, I can hear the voices and rustling and scuffling of the Viet Cong's movements. They are close. Only a thin wooden wall separates us. They are so close. How many of them—I don't know. Tens, hundreds, maybe thousands?

I can hear my own breathing, and a sense of panic strikes

me. I know Ba Noi told me to be very quiet and still, but each breath I take sounds so loud.

I tell myself: "Please breathe quieter. Please, nose, don't make that wheezing noise. Please, body, please, don't shake. The Viet Cong are a few steps away. Body, be still. Please, body, do not shake, do not gasp, and do not move. I can't let them find me."

The deafening noise of gunfire pierces my ears. My head vibrates with each blast. How many guns are out there? The crack of gunfire is coming from every direction, and bullets tear through the bedroom walls.

Are the walls shaking? Is the house falling apart? I can feel the vibration all around me.

The loudest explosion causes the house to shake more than ever. People are screaming outside the walls. Someone is in pain. My mind is going crazy. Is it Ba Noi? Where are you, Ba Noi? Please, hurry. Ba Noi, you should be here any second, and you will pull me close, and all the sounds will go away.

Seconds have passed, minutes have passed, hours have passed—I don't know anymore—and still Ba Noi is not here. I am no longer in control. I can't be still. My body won't stop shaking. I want to yell out, "Ba Noi, where are you? Please tell me where you are." But I know I need to be quiet.

The house continues to shake, the ground continues to rumble and blasts of gunfire and screeching voices beyond the thin wooden walls surround me. I am afraid. I don't know what to do except cry like a baby. Cry and think only of Ba Noi. I need to find her. Is she hurt?

Please, Buddha, protect Ba Noi. I sit as a lotus and chant for Buddha to protect Ba Noi. The ghastly noise continues. I can't let go and think of nothing. Thoughts of Ba Noi are still in my head. I must find her.

I climb out of the dugout. On my stomach and elbows, I start crawling toward her cot. Sounds of gunfire are even louder—behind me, in front of me, all around me. Several bullets strike the wooden walls close by me. I flinch. I want to yell out, "Ba Noi! Please, I am scared! Where are you? Please, come for me. Please, come."

No sign of her, only the horrific noises on the other side of the walls.

It feels like forever, but finally I reach the cot. I raise my head and reach above it to touch the mattress to feel for Ba Noi. My hands feel nothing but the cotton sheets.

I raise myself up completely and kneel on the ground beside Ba Noi's bed.

Ba Noi is not here.

My heart starts to race, and each beat feels like a hammer is pounding inside my chest, my head, and my body. Where is she?

I am disobeying Ba Noi, but I cannot keep quiet. I whimper, then hysterically wail. I call out: "Ba Noi, where are you? Come for me." I roll under her bed, not knowing what to do next.

I hear her voice. "Oanh, stay where you are."

I stay under the bed but reach my arms out as far as I can to feel for her. She sounds so close. I extend my arms out to her voice.

There she is. She slides under the bed and holds me so tight, I almost can't breathe, but I don't mind. Being wrapped in her arms feels so wonderful.

Ba Noi puts her hand to my mouth to signal me to stop crying. I stop crying, but then the hiccups start.

The gunfire subsides for a moment. Ba Noi's breath feels warm on my ear as she instructs me to stay close to her. We are going to crawl out from under the bed now. We quickly make our way across the dirt floor and into the dugout.

The gunfire, shouting and movements begin again behind our wall as Ba Noi and I cower in one corner of the dugout. I lean my whole body against hers. My head presses against her warm chest.

Ba Noi whispers: "I am sorry. I couldn't come to the dugout right away. I tried, but too many bullets were coming through our walls. Oanh, promise me, the next time if I don't come right away, you won't leave the dugout. Promise me you will not leave the dugout."

I turn to face her and whisper back: "Yes, Ba Noi. I am sorry. I was scared. I heard someone screaming in pain. I thought it was you. I promise I won't leave the dugout next time."

Ba Noi gently presses my head on her chest again. She starts chanting in a soft, soothing voice. She is not mad at me. I will be very good next time. I will be very quiet, and I will not leave the dugout.

The rapid beating of her heart blends beautifully with her rhythmic chant. It is very comforting as I feel the warmth of her hand patting my back. Instantly, all else around me fades away.

At other times, the dugout gave me a feeling of suffocation and death. Right now, it is our haven. I welcome the coolness of the fresh dirt as my feet dig into it.

As we await the promise of morning's calm, there is only the heartbeat of Ba Noi, her soothing chants, and her special scent—jasmine.

They remind me of a drawing I have seen—in one of my schoolbooks—of Chinese warriors dressed in their war clothes, heavily armed and looking fierce.

AMERICAN SOLDIERS

What is all that thundering and rumbling under our feet? The earth is shaking! The ground is moving! What is happening?

"The Americans are coming, the Americans are coming," a few of the village children shout as they run down the dirt road in excitement.

Ba Noi and I rush out to the road, too. Yes, the Americans are here!

Under our feet, the vibrations are getting stronger and stronger as the American troops march toward us. Ba Noi pulls me away from the dirt road. We stand very close to our mango tree, and there before our eyes is the beginning of a parade. American music, very loud American music, plays.

I love parades, especially the Chinese Lunar New Year Parade. People dress in costumes of a big red dragon and dance down the dirt roads. They make music with drums and gongs, and they pop firecrackers. It is a very festive time. We celebrate for days and days.

In the American parade, no one dresses in dragon costumes. The gigantic American soldiers on foot are dressed in dark green uniforms and big black boots, and a few have heavy metal green helmets on their heads.

Ba Noi and I step back behind the mango tree as they continue to march toward us. The American music gets louder and louder.

Oh my goodness! These American soldiers are strange and kind of scary looking. They look very different than those who came to our village a few months ago. The soldiers who came with Miss Le were nice and gentle. They had grand smiles, showing shiny white teeth as they gave us medical checkups to help us stay healthy. And afterward, we were given little gifts, which I still keep in my treasure chest.

Ba Noi must know that I am uncomfortable with these American soldiers. She takes my hand and holds it firmly.

One of the soldiers has a face with dark marks drawn under his eyes, and another has skin as dark as the black water buffalo. Some wear belts on their chests and waists with all kinds of things hanging off them—bullets, knives, and round metal things.

And, they all carry big guns! Some of the guns have lots of bullets hanging on them.

They remind me of a drawing I have seen—in one of my schoolbooks—of Chinese warriors dressed in their war clothes, heavily armed and fierce looking.

It's so hot and muggy. I wonder how the Americans stay cool with all the stuff they have on.

As the soldiers walk by us, some wave hello. Some greet us in Vietnamese. A few smile at us, but I do not see any shiny white teeth. Oh, one of them just spit some yucky, black tobacco close to our mango tree.

The soldiers talk and laugh with each other. A few smoke cigarettes and pass them around among themselves.

Two or three Vietnamese soldiers march along with the Americans. They look similar to the soldiers at the military compound across the streets. They are not outfitted like these Americans. The Vietnamese soldiers wear sandals or regular shoes, no big black boots.

I can't imagine that the American with the tangerine hair,

brown spots on his face and strange blue eyes—the one who gave me a shot in my arm so I could stay healthy and who said I had beautiful eyes—would be with these soldiers.

Then I see something that I know Ba Noi will not allow me to do. A couple of children in the village walk and talk with the American soldiers. They call out, "GI! GI! GI!"

The soldiers give them candies. One boy asks one for money, too. The soldier looks like he is having fun with the little boy. He gives the little boy some cigarettes instead.

Other children stand along the dirt road and yell, "GI, candy! GI, candy!" The soldiers are very amused by them and toss candies to them. Still other children run after the soldiers, begging for more candies.

Ba Noi looks at me and gives me a look to let me know that she does not like the children asking for candies and money from strangers. I dare not leave her side. She does not have to worry about me.

Next come the jeeps and trucks. The music blasts away as the vehicles approach us. The trucks mostly are filled with American soldiers, but there are a few Vietnamese soldiers, too. There are three or four trucks, each loaded with soldiers, talking, laughing and teasing each other.

Some soldiers wave to us from their jeeps and trucks. Ba Noi never waves back. She does not even nod her head to greet them, nor does she look straight at them. She just stands still. I follow Ba Noi's example and stand still, too.

I have never seen anything like this. A green metal monster moving machine creeps up closer to us; it makes me shudder. The vibrations from the ground become stronger. It feels like I am being shaken off the earth. The monster is like a ferocious green dragon. It has many wheels, like the dragon with many legs. Instead of a mouth filled with fire, soldiers emerge from the big green monster's mouth, which has the biggest gun attached to it. This gun is bigger than any gun at the military compound across the dirt road.

An American soldier pops his head and shoulders out of the mouth of this thing. He sways and shakes his head to the loud music. He waves to another soldier in a different green metal monster moving machine behind him. The monsters pass by us unaware of the rumbling of earth beneath them and the goose bumps forming on my arms and legs.

One more truck of GIs trails behind.

Our eyes follow the parade. The vibrations get weaker and the music becomes softer as we watch the parade getting smaller and smaller as it moves farther and farther from our mango tree, pass my school, pass my uncle's orchard, and toward the rice paddies. The parade fades away, leaving only a cloud of dust. The crowd dissipates.

I ask Ba Noi: "Where are they going? Where does the parade end?"

"Oanh, this is not a parade. The Americans are going beyond the rice paddies." She gently shakes her head, and a worried look appears on her face as her eyes follow the cloud of dust near the rice paddies. "They are going to find the Viet Cong."

In a gush, the fresh memories of the Viet Cong behind our wall, the sounds of gunfire, the screams of pain and the smell of the fresh dirt in the dugout under my bed fill my mind. How frightened I was, especially when Ba Noi was not at my side.

The vibrations disturb my thoughts. So many trucks filled with American GIs, so many big monster green metal moving machines, so many huge guns—yes they will find the Viet Cong. No longer will we have to hide in the dugout. Beyond the rice paddies, they will find all the Viet Cong—I hope.

I give the GIs a little wave as I look toward the rice paddies.

As he moves closer to us, I see stains of dried and fresh blood on one of his pant legs.

PARADE OF THE DEAD

I don't remember how many days, weeks or months it has been since we saw the American GIs parading through our village on their way beyond the rice paddies.

I have been thinking about them, especially at night before I close my eyes. I feel safer knowing that so many American GIs with the big guns and the big machines are way beyond the rice paddies looking for the Viet Cong.

It has been quiet around our village. The Viet Cong have not battled with the South Vietnamese soldiers from behind our bedroom walls at night. Ba Noi and I have not had to hide in the dugout.

My fear of the dugout has almost gone away. The last time we had to hide in the dugout, I discovered it is a shelter. I was unsafe when I crawled out from it to look for Ba Noi. But when I found her and together we safely made our way back to the hole where Ba Noi soothed me, the sounds of machine guns with bullets ricocheting on our wooden walls all disappeared. We were safe in our hole.

Today, word has gotten to us that the American soldiers are coming out from beyond the rice paddies. I am so excited. I have been waiting anxiously for them. Perhaps Ba Noi will let me go up to them this time. I won't ask for candies or money. I just want to thank them for going beyond the rice paddies.

Again, Ba Noi and I stand by the mango tree to watch for the American soldiers. I am waiting for the first sign of them, for some of the other children running down the dirt road chanting in excitement that the GIs are coming, the GIs are coming.

But there is no sign of the soldiers. Ba Noi leaves me by the mango tree. She is in the kitchen area warming our lunch. I am just going to wait here until they come.

While waiting, my mind wanders to my mother. Where has she been? When was she here last? It must have been months and months. She must be very busy with work.

I look down the dirt road, beyond my school, beyond my uncle's orchard.

Yes, I see them coming! Some of the Vietnamese soldiers across the road are coming out from their compound. They also wait for the American soldiers. Other people start to gather around, too.

Huh, where are the other children? Why are they not calling out, "The Americans are coming?"

Something is different. It doesn't feel like the first time I saw them parading by our house. A dark gray cloud forms above them.

The Americans are getting closer, now. I am getting a clear view of them. Just two or three soldiers are on foot—not as many as the first time. No, these soldiers cannot be the same GIs we saw in the parade. They do not sway to music but rather drag their feet with each step. The music is not playing like before.

The dark gray cloud hovers above all of us. It must have followed them beyond the rice paddies. The soldiers walk as if that dark cloud burst into one of the monster machines with the big gun. The weight of the monster machine crushed them, crushed their spirits.

The American soldiers' helmets, clothes and boots are

caked with yucky mud and dust. One soldier is limping. As he moves closer to us, I see stains of dried and fresh blood on one of his pant legs.

I raise my head and look at his face. I do not see gleaming white teeth, a playful grin or teasing eyes. I see lips bruised and puffy, blood smeared across his dirty face, and eyes stoic and cold.

This is not the time to thank him for going beyond the rice paddies.

I feel the glare of another set of eyes, another American soldier just a couple of steps behind. He does not have his metal helmet on. His hair is curly with a reddish glare to it. He reminds me so much of the American with the tangerine hair, brownish orange spots on his face, and strange beautiful blue eyes—the nice one who gave me a shot in my arm so I can stay healthy and told me that I have big beautiful eyes. The soldier stares at me, straight into my eyes. I stare back and realize that he was not staring at me but at something beyond me, perhaps something beyond the rice paddies.

The dark gray cloud turns into many huge dark clouds. As they multiply, the gray bubbles into black gloom and spreads everywhere.

As this soldier passes by me, his eyes dart rapidly. His face twitches as if, for a second, a loud noise or commotion has surprised him. There is no gleaming smile, just a little blood, because he is biting his lip.

No, this is not a good time to thank him, either.

Ba Noi comes out of the kitchen and joins me by the mango tree. A couple of boys from the village walk up to the GIs. One boy, older than me, holds out his hand and asks for something. I cannot hear what he wants. He starts to reach for one GI's pants pocket.

In a gruff voice, the soldier tells him in Vietnamese, "Go, go, go away." And with the end of his big, long gun he pushes the boy away.

The boy falls down and lets out a little cry. He runs away toward Ba Noi and me. As he retreats behind us, he says something obscene about the soldier.

The GI, with his face glazed and eyes cold, continues to pick up one foot after another. He moves forward as if nothing has happened, as if he is under the dark cloud by himself.

A couple of jeeps, trucks and monster green metal moving machines follow the soldiers. Everything is smeared with brownish black mud. As the monster machines roll by, pieces of mud fall off.

The trucks are not filled with soldiers like before. Not all those who paraded beyond the rice paddies are returning in these mucky trucks.

The people from the village are very quiet. Some bow their heads low as the soldiers pass by. The Vietnamese soldiers across the road from us shake their heads in despair and head back slowly into their compound.

The dark gray cloud of gloom and sadness hovers above, and a misty rain begins to sprinkle us. The American soldiers as well as the people from the village, Ba Noi, the boy behind us and I all stand in the same rain and under the same dark clouds.

Where are the Viet Cong? Did the Americans find them? And where are the rest of the American GIs? Are they still beyond the rice paddies?

Days pass and the faces of the soldiers still haunt me and appear in my sleep. I look to the sky, still washed with the gray clouds of the monsoon rain. The season seems longer and my mother seems farther away.

I will chant for the gray clouds to go away, for the rain to stop, for the sun to shine, and for Mother to come and grace me with her beautiful smile.

I saw my Ba Noi—her eyes moist, smiling so lovingly as the tears rolled down her cheeks.

RIDE TO SAIGON

Sitting in the back of the taxi with my mother, we ride to Saigon.

It seems unbearably long. Many confusing thoughts float through my head. I can hear my mother speak, but the sound isn't clear. It is distant and muffled.

"Life will be wonderful in America."

I nod my head.

I am getting queasy; I poke my head out the window for fresh air. My mind plays back the events of the day. How could it be? This morning I was playing and looking forward to a visit from my mother, and this afternoon my clothes and a few belongings are in the trunk of the taxi.

The taxi is taking us away from Ba Noi, away from the only home I know. My home and Ba Noi's, made of thin wooden slats with the big mango tree out front, under which the Buddha monks cured me from all the painful bubbles. My home, in which Ba Noi made me cool mint juice when the days became so hot, muggy and uncomfortable. My home, with my high straw bed and the dugout under it, giving Ba Noi and me shelter when gunfire burst out.

This is not happening. Mother, where have you been for so long? And just like that, you pop out of nowhere and my belongings are thrown into the trunk of this taxi. Ba Noi, I don't want to leave my home. I don't want to leave you.

I look out the window, breathe calmly and chant silently,

like a Lotus. Now, I remember, there were other times when I was in a taxi with my mother.

One morning she came early and said she had the whole day to spend with me. A full day with my mother! What a wonderful treat! A few hours at most are what I usually had with Mother.

That time, she surprised me with an unexpected trip to the beach in Vung Tau. It didn't matter to me where we went. I was happy just to be with her.

My mother was so playful that day. We talked and laughed as we tried to catch all the sand crabs at the beach. The crabs were very tiny but extremely fast. In a couple of hours, we caught maybe eight or ten. Finally, we released them and watched them dig back into the cool wet sand.

Then Mother and I walked hand-in-hand along the edge of the warm ocean water. As the water surged in and rolled out, we watched our feet disappear and reappear.

My trance is broken. The taxi is bouncing up and down and makes loud crashing noises each time it lands on the bumpy road as it speeds along. The driver seems amused. I fly out of the seat and hit my head. I think I am going to throw up.

"Mother, please stop the car." I beg.

Mother shouts for the driver to pull over. She grabs my hand and helps me out. She pulls my hair back as I spit out the last of the awful taste in my mouth. I am feeling better.

We get back into the smelly taxi, and the driver pulls onto the road hastily, leaving a cloud of dust behind.

Mother yells at the driver, "Are you crazy-in-the-head? Slow down or my daughter will get sick all over you."

She looks at me caringly and asks me to sit closer to her. She moves my hair away from my face and starts to comb it with her fingers. I scoot closer, lean back and start to relax. I close my eyes and remember another time when Mother graced me with her presence.

It was early afternoon. I was standing next to her, scratching my head as she talked to Ba Noi. The itching wouldn't go away. I continued to ferociously scratch and scratch. Mother gave me a weird look. She stopped talking to Ba Noi and leaned her body and face away from me.

Mother asked Ba Noi if I had lice. Ba Noi looked at me. I couldn't help it. I scratched, scratched and scratched.

Ba Noi said, "It could be so." She explained to Mother that she had been washing my hair regularly. A few days ago, though, school had reopened. It would have been possible for me to get lice from one of the other children.

Ba Noi asked me if the itching was getting worse.

I nodded yes.

I tried not to scratch. I didn't want to make a big deal about it. Mother is here to see me, to be with me. I didn't want to spend precious time talking about the lice on my head. But those ugly, grotesque lice must have been biting into my skull and brain. They were sucking all my blood. I couldn't stop scratching.

Mother got up and quickly moved away from me. She asked Ba Noi where the nearest hair cut place was located, and the next thing I knew I was sitting on a small wooden chair getting my head shaved. I was completely bald.

Afterward, we got into a taxi. For the whole ride back to the house of Ba Noi, I couldn't help but rub my head. It felt so strange, so smooth, so soft, but so cold and naked.

The taxi stopped in front of the house, and Mother and I got out. Ba Noi came to greet us. She looked at me with a sympathetic smile as she stroked my bald head.

Mother announced that she must get back to Saigon for work. She gave me a kiss on the cheek and told me that I was still pretty. I think, by then, my left hand was glued to the top of my head.

She took off her lovely little gold chain necklace and placed it around my neck. I think she also slipped some money into Ba Noi's hand, and away she went.

Ba Noi laid her hand on my shoulder while I waved goodbye to Mother, the taxi leaving a trail of dust as it sped away.

As naked as I felt with not even an itsy bitsy little fuzzy hair on my head, I smiled. Mother had just graced me—with the necklace that she wore, with her smile, with her kiss, with her sweet scent and with her forever vivacious presence.

I jerk, sit up and open my eyes wide as the taxi driver honks the horn. Oh my, so many scooters, bicycles, and automobiles. Their horns are blasting all around, and people waving their arms and fingers angrily as they shout obscene words to each other.

Mother looks down at me with her beautiful face and says: "Daughter, we are almost home. We are in Saigon, and in two more streets you will meet your new American father."

I must have fallen asleep; it takes me a few seconds to recollect all that has happened. Oh, I am in a taxi with Mother next to me. We are in Saigon. In months, we will be in America. Mother has said that life will be wonderful in America.

I always have wanted to be with my mother. I have missed her so much. Then why, why, is my heart now deep in sadness? I turn my face away from Mother and look out the rear window of the taxi. The image of Ba Noi appears.

I had perched on my knees on the back seat of the taxi to look out the rear window as we drove away. I saw my Ba Noi—her eyes moist, smiling so lovingly as the tears rolled down her cheeks.

From now on he is only twelve years old, not fourteen.

SAIGON

I am so afraid.

In my mother's villa in Saigon, I am meeting my stepfather for the first time. He looks very much like the nice American who came to our village to give us children shots in our arms so we could stay healthy. I can't believe it! He has the same tangerine hair, beautiful blue eyes and smile with gleaming white teeth.

But I can't go up to him.

Mother says, "Go, go, give your new father a hug."

My heart is beating so fast, and my hands are sweating like crazy. I move slowly toward him. When I'm two steps away, suddenly he bends down, reaches out, whisks me up, and scoops me into the air.

He holds me close to him. My face is right next to his. He is so tall. I am way up high from the floor. He looks at me straight into my eyes and says in broken Vietnamese, "Oanh, I am so happy to have you here with us."

It is a little hard to understand him. He must see my shock and confusion, because he repeats himself.

I still do not say anything. I want to, but the words will not come out of my mouth. I am too afraid to look at him, and instead I cast my eyes to the floor.

Mother repeats what he said.

I nod my head that I understand and say, "Thank you."

***

Mother tells me she met my new American stepfather a little over two years ago. They got married here in Saigon quickly because the American Army had given him orders to go home to America.

I don't remember Ba Noi telling me that Mother had married an American GI and left Vietnam with him. Now, I understand why I did not see her for a very long time.

They had been living in America for a few months when Mother became very depressed. She finally confessed that she was very sad because she missed her country and most of all because she missed her children. She told him she must leave and go back to Vietnam. She was very sorry for not telling him the truth.

Mother said my new stepfather was so wonderful because he promised they would go back to Vietnam together. He told her he loved her and wanted to be with her no matter what. He also said he understood why she didn't tell him the truth when they met.

So Stepfather went to the American Army and requested orders to go back to Vietnam.

Now, here they are, gathering the family together so we can all go to America and have a wonderful family and good future.

Mother says that our new stepfather's mother and father also are very nice people. They are looking forward to meeting us children. We are going to stay with them for a little while when we arrive in America.

**

Awaking, I hear voices. One of them is a little boy's. It is a baby-like voice, so cute and adorable. I take a minute or so to get my head straight.

Yesterday, I was in Bien Hoa with Ba Noi, waking up to the

sounds of the rooster's cockle-doodle-do and the smell of sweet anise in the Pho for breakfast. This morning, where am I?

Oh, yes, the ride in the taxi with Mother, my new American stepfather—the gentle giant—and the big city of Saigon.

When I woke up in the cab yesterday, two streets away from my new home, I couldn't believe it. There were so many people, big houses, even bigger buildings with window after window stacked higher and higher to the sky, shops, markets, scooters, bicycles, cars, jeeps and trucks everywhere. Honk! Honk! Honk! Honk! was all I heard.

I had been to Saigon a couple of times before with my mother, but I didn't remember it being so crowded and noisy.

Even now, waking up inside a house with four actual walls and locked doors, I can hear the distant honks from the streets.

Oh, the baby-like voice. Here it is again. It is so cute.

Slowly, I rise and find my way to the voices. I see an adorable little boy with chubby cheeks and the biggest, roundest, light bright brown eyes. His skin is ivory toned, just like the beautiful tusk on an elephant.

Looking up at me, in a sweet little voice, he asks an old woman, "Is this my sister?"

The old woman, who has a small, very round face and thinning gray hair that is much shorter than my Ba Noi's, comes toward me with a smile. What black teeth she has. They look like the teeth of the people who chewed tobacco in my village.

She reaches out to touch my cheek with her right hand, and I see her brown-stained fingertips. They feel rough and have a familiar, unpleasant odor.

A faded picture surfaces in my head. The body of an old man on a hard wooden bed is before me.

Mother had taken me to the house where she was raised. I still can hear the puttering motor on the little rickety boat that was just big enough to carry the man operating it, Mother and me across the big brown river to get to her family's house.

There was something very serene yet dark about this journey. The humming of the motor filled my ears, and I saw our crossing clearly— the brown water all around us and the dark green lushness of the land on the other side of the river as it finally came into view.

We jumped out of the boat onto the slushy, muddy riverbank, and then we climbed up a heavily vegetated hill to the house of Ba Ngoai and Ong Ngoai.

At the top of the little hill was a vast pink grapefruit orchard. Its scent was so aromatic and mesmerizing. I just wanted to stand there and whiff it all in. Mother was slowing down, too, and for a few seconds, she stopped and smelled the scent with me.

As we approached the house, a dark cloud settled in and appeared to linger right above it.

We entered the house, and right away I smelled something moldy. The house gave me a very eerie feeling, so I stayed close to the entryway as Mother went toward an altar to greet an old woman, my Ba Ngoai.

The house was very dim, especially because of the dark cloud lingering above it. It had one big open room, and in the back was the altar, adorned with several Buddha statues, pictures of ancestors, incense and fruit.

Mother and Ba Ngoai embraced and spoke to each other in low voices. Ba Ngoai looked at me and nodded her head.

Mother then raised her voice to me. "What is wrong with you? Come, come and greet your Ba Ngoai."

I unwillingly and haltingly walked toward the altar. In front of the old woman, I bowed my head.

She opened her mouth and said, "Don't be a crybaby." Saliva formed on each corner of her mouth. Her teeth were black.

From the altar area, I was barely able to see a tall wooden bed at the very back corner of the house. On it lay Ong Ngoai. He was nothing more than skin and bones, and he moaned as if he were in so much pain.

The scent of the grapefruit orchard had disappeared, and the strong, heavy odor of Tiger Balm began to suffocate me.

Mother instructed me to be good and not make too much noise, because Ong Ngoai was resting. She asked me to stay put as she and Ba Ngoai tip-toed over to his bedside. I did not follow them; instead, I headed back to the entryway, to the light.

Awakening me from this eerie picture is the cheerful, sweet, adorable voice of the little boy. He asks a second time, "Is this my big sister?"

Ba Ngoai replies, "Yes, this is your big sister, Oanh."

She puts a small piece of meat in her mouth and chews it several times. With her fingers, she takes the meat out of her mouth and inserts it into his.

Happily, he chews it and then looks at me with those amazing eyes. "Hi, Big Sister. Are you staying with us? You can sleep with me and Ba Ngoai."

From this moment on, Hung is my cheerful, sweet, adorable little brother forever.

***

We have been so busy preparing for our departure to America.

My older brother, Dung, and I are walking to class for our English lesson. I think I am doing quite well learning the new language. I am able to say words like hello, thank you, chair, table, pencil, watch, you, I, mother, father, brother, sister, and crazy. I can even say whole sentences: "How are you?" "Today, I am good."

Some words are easier than others. I cannot easily say well the words with Ls and Rs in them. Dung is having an even harder time learning them. But our teacher is a Vietnamese man who has been to America, so he knows how to speak English very well.

***

I love walking to different places in Saigon with my brother. It is the best time for us to practice the English words that we have just learned in class.

I ask him if he thinks it is easier to communicate with our American stepfather now that we have learned how to speak English. My brother, who is very wise, says that we probably speak English the same way that our new American stepfather speaks Vietnamese. We both laugh.

Dung is so much fun to be with. He knows the big city and all the shortcuts to lots of wonderful places.

He has taken me to see a movie at the big movie house, where the moving pictures are shown on a wall screen. The pictures are humongous, making the scary movie about the bad people going to hell even scarier. All the ghosts and demons look very real, and at times I think they will jump out off the wall screen. I don't like the movie, but it is fun spending the day with my big brother.

Dung has extra money after the movie finishes, so he buys me candies and chewing gum. As we walk back home, he shows me how to blow big bubbles with the gum.

He tells me that Mother and our American stepfather had to pay someone to change his age on the official birth certificate document. From now on he is only twelve years old, not fourteen. At his real age, the South Vietnamese Army would not allow him to leave our country, because in one more year he would be old enough to join them and fight the Viet Cong.

There was a time when he wanted to join the army, but

not now. Now Mother has gotten us so excited about living in America.

***

My mother is right. As the months go by, I find that our new American stepfather is very nice, kind and gentle. He never yells at us. When he comes home from work, he gives Mother a kiss, greets all of us and even asks us how we are doing. He brings us little presents from his work.

Today, I get to see where Stepfather works—the American military hospital in Saigon. It is my turn to have a checkup with the American doctor before we go to America.

This is the first time that Stepfather and I are alone together, and I love it! He speaks to me the whole time. He holds my hand as he introduces me to all the people at his work.

Our visit with the American doctor, yet another American with tangerine hair and amazing blue eyes, is much longer than the visits Ba Noi and I had with Mr. Doctor in our village in Bien Hoa. The American doctor checks almost every part of my body. I even have to give him a sample of my urine.

Stepfather and the American doctor must be telling funny jokes to each other because they laugh a lot. I am very shy, but I try to give big smiles now and then when they laugh. Oh my! Now, I am really embarrassed. Stepfather says that the American doctor told him that I have the most gorgeous big almond shape eyes he has seen and I will be a very beautiful young lady one day. I am too embarrassed and cannot look at the doctor or my Stepfather. I keep my head low and give a little smile as I remember the first Americans I saw whom came to our village to give us medical checkups.

I am feeling like the most beautiful princess in the whole wide world. It is such a fantastic day being with Stepfather.

***

Our stay in Saigon has gone by very quickly. Everyone has been so busy. With so many new surprises and new things to learn, I haven't had much time to think about my old school, the mean Chinese girl next door, Ba Noi or the Viet Cong behind our house.

Both Mother and Stepfather are working hard to earn extra money for our trip. I overheard them talking one night about the paperwork to get us approved to come to America. It is not easy to get; it takes a long time, and it is expensive. They have to pay many people extra money to process our paperwork.

It is good that Mother and Stepfather don't smoke or drink much alcohol. For extra money, they can sell the American cigarettes and alcohol that they are able to buy to others.

Ba Ngoai helps out with making dinner and taking care of my little brother.

***

Boom! Boom! What is going on? It is very dark. We are all in our beds, but Mother is telling us to come and huddle together in her and Stepfather's room. We need to take cover.

The loud booms repeat over and over! From a distance somewhere in Saigon, bombs are exploding! The Viet Cong are here in Saigon, too.

Ba Ngoai is soothing Little Brother. He is very scared and crying.

Memory of the dugout floods my mind. I am scared, too, but Ba Noi appears. Yes, I remember, be a Lotus. I reach out and take my little brother's hand and place it in mine. I sit still, breathe and softly chant. Jasmine fills the air. Morning will come soon.

***

Mother is taking me in a taxi to visit Thu Ha, the youngest of her four children. Thu Ha is around three or four years old. Thu Ha's father is an American GI who left my mother stranded when she was pregnant. He went home to America, and Mother has not heard from him since.

During our ride to the house of Thu Ha, Mother tells me that Thu Ha will not be coming to America with us. Mother explains that she could not take care of a baby and work. At the same time, Mother's uncle and his wife had been desperately wanting a baby for a long time. They are good and loving people, so at that time, Mother felt that leaving Thu Ha with them was the best thing to do.

I have a really strange feeling here at Thu Ha's house. I will wait for Mother in the front part of the house, which is divided by a screen of long stranded beads.

Mother and Thu Ha's new mother and father are talking behind the screen. I can't really hear the conversation, but I do hear a lot of crying.

I peek through the strands and see a beautiful little girl. She looks very much like my baby brother. Her face is most precious with the cutest nose, the pinkest full lips and shining, light yellowish brown hair. She is busy running back and forth between her new mother and father.

The crying turns into sobs. All three of them—Mother and Thu Ha's new mother and father—are sobbing loudly. Frightened, Thu Ha walks around and hides behind her new mother.

Mother stands up and walks through the strands of beads. I follow her, and we leave the house. The taxi is still waiting for us. Quickly, we climb into the back seat, and Mother asks the driver to go.

Patting her face with a handkerchief, Mother wipes away tears.

But more tears flow.

"I want to be a good mother, a good person. I came back—back to get all my children. Thu Ha, I won't forget you. I will come back for you."

I inch closer to Mother, pat her hand and lean my head on her shoulder. She cries some more as the taxi turns a corner and takes us away from Thu Ha.

***

It is a happy and a sad day.

Today, we are at the Saigon International Airport. Mother and Ba Ngoai are crying. Hung, my little brother, is fidgeting as Ba Ngoai tries to hold him back from running off somewhere. Stepfather is very busy with all of our suitcases and paperwork. Big Brother is trying to help Stepfather.

My heart is skipping every other beat. Oh, I am so happy, excited and nervous at the same time. We are getting ready to board a huge airplane.

I told Big Brother the other day I was scared to go on an airplane. He said not to worry; he would take care of me. He hasn't flown before either, but he is not afraid.

Mother and Ba Ngoai are crying a little louder.

Ba Ngoai looks so sad and old. She is not coming with us. She keeps repeating, "Oh, God, my little baby, my little baby boy. Oh God, take care of him. Take care of him." She is crying to Mother and is now clutching onto Little Brother.

Mother cries as she tells Ba Ngoai: "He is my son. Don't worry. I will take care of him. Please visit Thu Ha now and then. Tell her I will not forget her. I love her. I will send money."

Mother takes my hand and asks, "Oanh, are you ready? Are you ready to fly across the ocean to America?"

"Yes, Mother. I am ready."

We line up to go outside to board the big airplane.

It is hard for us to get comfortable in our seats. The pretty ladies are very helpful. They give Mother little bags for us. Mother hands them to us and says, "It is for you just in case you feel sick and need to throw up."

I guess she remembers when I was very sick in the taxi rides.

Stepfather lets me sit on his lap for a few minutes so I can look out the window more easily. He has told us that his mother and father still have the Christmas tree up and that there are presents under the tree for all of us. It is now February and they have been waiting anxiously for us to come.

Presents, Christmas—what is it all about? I don't really know, but from the sound of it, many good things are waiting for us.

Stepfather gently slips me off his lap and buckles me into the seat by myself. Bending over so he does not hit his head, he shuffles out of the row of seats and over to Mother. They kiss, and he tells her he will be coming home shortly. Stepfather is not making the trip with us, because the American Army will not allow him to return home yet. He is supposed to join us in a few weeks.

Stepfather tells Dung, Hung and me that he will miss us. He asks us to be good and says that he will see us soon. He turns and kisses Mother again and then walks down the aisle and off the plane.

The plane pulls away from the gate. Oh, the takeoff! The sounds from the airplane are very loud, and the vibrations are a little nerve-racking. It is all so terrifying and yet thrilling at the same time.

I think my heart just skipped a few beats. Little Brother Hung is making sounds like the airplane and is oblivious to any of the noises and turbulence. Big Brother Dung has his eyes closed and his arms crossed over each other.

He must have sensed me watching him, because he opens his eyes and gives me one of his crooked smiles as he nods his head, like all is good. He does not look afraid, I don't think, so I am not afraid, either. I smile back at him.

Mother is smiling, too. She is happy.

We are up so high! I look out the window and down below. The lush green shores so magnificently outline the winding, murky brown river. There are several water buffalos in the beautiful rice fields so perfectly lined out into little squares. Barely can I see the people below.

As the image gets smaller and smaller, I think of the river back in my village under the bridge, where the home of Ba Noi is—where my home is. I take a deep breath and can almost smell the fresh limes from my uncle's orchard.

The most beautiful and tranquil of all visions appear: Ba Noi, smiling at me, comforting me with her loving eyes. Ba Noi, breathing in the fresh morning dew as her arms gracefully flow in the air while she practices tai chi.

Oh, her calm, soothing voice; her soft chant.

It seems so long ago that we were together in the dugout under my straw bed. For a few seconds, as the airplane lifts us higher into the sky then levels out and its loud noise settles into a rhythm, I hear Ba Noi's rapid heartbeat blending beautifully with her soft chant, and the scent of jasmine surrounds and comforts me.

The brown river fades away. Puffy clouds appear. No signs of dark clouds—just soft, cottony white clouds.

A couple of teardrops roll down my cheeks, and I quickly wipe them away.

I love you Ba Noi. We will see each other again one day, I promise.

Made in the USA